William Sandys Wright Vaux

Persia

From the Earliest Period to the Arab conquest

William Sandys Wright Vaux

Persia

From the Earliest Period to the Arab conquest

ISBN/EAN: 9783744751858

Printed in Europe, USA, Canada, Australia, Japan

Cover: Foto ©ninafisch / pixelio.de

More available books at **www.hansebooks.com**

ANCIENT HISTORY

FROM THE MONUMENTS.

PERSIA.

ANCIENT HISTORY

FROM THE MONUMENTS.

I. EGYPT. From the earliest times to B. C. 300.
By S. BIRCH, LL. D.

II. ASSYRIA. From the earliest times to the fall of Nineveh.
By GEORGE SMITH, of the British Museum.

III. PERSIA. From the earliest period to the Arab Conquest.
By W. S. W. VAUX, M. A. F. R. S.

In this series we have a compact but popular presentation of the highly important results of recent archæological investigation. The annals of Egypt, Assyria and Persia, as derived from the monuments and from the cuneiform inscriptions generally, are of the greatest importance to understanding the development of human civilization and the tendency of religious thought. Besides this there has been brought out a mass of evidence and illustration on manners and customs, language and literature, tending to throw light on the earlier books of the Bible, a knowledge of which is indispensable to every well-informed man. This has heretofore been practically inaccessible because of the recondite manner in which it has been discussed. Each of these volumes has been prepared by specialists who are masters of their respective departments.

Each volume handsomely illustrated. Small 12mo. Cloth. Price, $1.00.

⁂ SENT POST-PAID, UPON RECEIPT OF PRICE, BY

SCRIBNER, ARMSTRONG & CO.,

New York.

ROCK OF BEHISTAN.

ANCIENT HISTORY

FROM THE MONUMENTS.

PERSIA

FROM THE

EARLIEST PERIOD TO THE ARAB CONQUEST.

BY

W. S. W. VAUX, M. A., F. R. S.

NEW YORK:
SCRIBNER, ARMSTRONG & CO.
1876.

CONTENTS.

LIST OF DYNASTIES..................................Page vi.
INTRODUCTION......................................Page vii.

CHAPTER I.

Cyrus—Crœsus—War in North-east Asia—Fall of Babylon—Tomb of Cyrus—Cambyses—Pseudo-Bardes—Darius—Campaign in Scythia—Home at Susa—Inscription and Coin of Pythagoras—Burning of Sardis—Second Invasion of Europe—Marathon..Page 16

CHAPTER II.

Xerxes—Canal of Athos—Thermopylæ—Salamis—Artaxerxes I.—Darius II.—Artaxerxes II.—Cyrus the Younger—Ochus—Darius III.—Alexander—Graneikus—Issus—Visit to Jerusalem—Arbela..Page 46

CHAPTER III.

Daniel—Darius the Mede..................................Page 73

CHAPTER IV.

Tomb of Cyrus—Inscriptions of Darius—Behistân—Vân, &c.—Inscriptions of Xerxes—Artaxerxes, &c.—Persepolis—Istakhr—Susa—Tomb of Darius..................................Page 87

CHAPTER V.

Arsacidæ—Arsakes I—Tiridates I—Artabanus I—Mithradates I—Phraates II—Scythian Invasion--Mithradates II—Progress of the Romans—Orodes—Crassus—Pompey—Antony—Tiridates, son of Vologases—Trajanus—Avidius Cassius—Severus—Artabanus—Battle of Nisibis..................................Page 123

CHAPTER VI.

Sassanidæ — Ardashír I. — Shahpúr I. —Valerian —Odænathus— Varahrán II.—Tiridates of Armenia—Galerius —Narses—Shahpúr II.—Zu'laktaf—Julian III.—Firúz I.—Nushírwán—Mauricius—Khosrú II.— Heraclius—Muhammed—Yezdigird III.— Muhammedan Conquest—Sassanian Monuments at Nakhsh-i-Rustám, Nakhsh-i-Regib, Shahpúr, Takht-i-Bostán — Mr. Thomas's interpretation of the inscriptions at Hajiábád.
Page 154

LIST OF DYNASTIES.

[Occasionally, these dates are only approximate: it has not been thought necessary to insert the names of rulers who ruled for less than a year.]

1. EARLY PERSIAN (ACHÆMENIDÆ).

	B.C.		B.C.		B.C.
Cambyses I		Xerxes	486	Artaxerxes III	
Cyrus	558	Artaxerxes I (Longimanus)	465	(Ochus)	359
Cambyses II	529			Arses	338-37
Pseudo-Smerdis (Bardes)	522	Darius II (Nothus)	425-24	Darius III (Codomannus)	336
Darius I	521	Artaxerxes II (Mnemon)	405	(Battle of Arbela)	331

2. ARSACIDÆ.

[Each of these princes bore also the dynastic title of Arsakes; hence Mithradates I is the same as Arsakes VI.]

	B.C.		B.C.		A.D.
Arsakes	about 250	Mithradates III	60	Pacorus II	78 ?
Tiridates I	247	Orodes I	56-55	Mithradates IV	107
Artabanus I	214	Phraates IV	37	Chosroes	113
Priapatius	196	Phraataces } dates doubtful		Vologases II	130
Phraates I	181	Orodes II }		Vologases III	149
Mithradates I	174	Vonones I...date doubtful		Vologases IV	191
Phraates II	136		A.D.	Vologases V	?
Artabanus II	128-7	Artabanus III	16	Artabanus IV	215 ?
Mithradates II	124	Gotarzes } dates doubtful		(Battle of Hormazd and death of Artabanus IV)	226
(Mnaskyres)	?	Vardanes }			
Sanatroces	76	Vonones II			
Phraates III	66	Vologases I	51		

SASSANIDÆ.

	A.D.		A.D.		A.D.
Ardashír I (Babekan)	226	Ardashír II	381	Kobád	488
Shahpúr I	240	Shahpúr III	385	Jamasp	498
Hormazd I	273	Varahrán IV (Kerman-Shah)	390	Khosru I (Nushirwan)	531
Varahrán I	274				
Varahrán II	277	Yezdigird I	404	Hormazd IV	579
Varahrán III	294	Varahrán V (Gaur)	420	Khosru II (Parviz)	591
Narses	294	Yezdigird II	448	Kobád II (Sheruyieh)	628
Hormazd II	303	Hormazd III	458	Yezdigird III	632
Shahpúr II (Zu'luktuf)	310	Firúz	458	(Overthrown by the Musulmans)	641
		Palash	484		

HISTORY OF PERSIA,

FROM THE EARLIEST PERIOD TO THE OVERTHROW OF ITS NATIVE DYNASTIES BY THE MUHAMMEDANS.

INTRODUCTION.

THE history of Persia, as generally understood, may be considered as a supplement to that of Assyria and Babylonia, the events that have made her most famous in antiquity having been achieved after the empire of the first had passed away, and the second had been subjugated by the Persians.

The small province of Persis (in the Bible *Paras*, in the native inscriptions *Parsa*), whence the name of Persia is derived, was bounded on the north by Media, on the south by the Persian Gulf and Indian Ocean, on the east by Caramania (Kerman), and on the west by Susiana. It was, indeed, nearly the same district as the modern Farsistan, the name of which is obviously derived from it; and in length and breadth not more than 450 and 250 miles respectively.

With regard to the population which occupied this district at the earliest *historical* period, it is certain from the Cuneiform inscriptions, that they were not the original dwellers in the district, but themselves immigrants, though it is not so certain whence. It would lead us too far a-field to discuss here the wide question of the settlement of the nations after the Biblical Flood, confirmed so remarkably as this is by Mr. George Smith's recent discoveries. Moreover, it is not possible to fill up, except conjecturally, many wide spaces, both of time and territory. Admitting, however, the existence of a Deluge, such as that recorded in Holy Writ, a long period must have elapsed before the different families of mankind had arranged themselves in the groups and in the districts we find them occupying at the dawn of history.

There are reasonable grounds for thinking the highlands of Central Asia the *historical* cradle of the Japhetic race; whether, with some writers, we conceive this mountainous region to be the Alpine plateau of Little Bokhara, or, with others, the great chain south and south-west of the Caspian Sea: the first theory suits best for a descent into India; the second for a migration into Europe.*

The former view, taken broadly, is confirmed by the early Persian traditions preserved in the two first chapters of the Vendidad, (though this compilation as we now have it, is very modern), an outline, in

* I venture to think it unwise to attempt, with Clinton and other learned chronologists, to space out the time occupied for each settlement or movement of the nations after the Flood, or to attempt to ascertain the number of the population of pre-historic Asia. For such speculations, we have, assuredly, no reliable data.

the judgment of Heeren, so evidently historical, as to require nothing but sufficient geographical knowledge for the identification of the places therein mentioned. Whether any of these traditional legends are really due to Zoroaster (Zaratrusthra), [indeed whether a Zoroaster ever lived], is of little importance: but this much, however, is certain that they enshrine fragments of the most ancient belief of the Persians. Thus, they describe as the original seat of the Persian race, a delicious country named *Eriene-Veedjo*, the first creation of Ormuzd, the Spirit of Good, with a climate of seven months of summer and five of winter. But Ahriman, the Spirit of Evil, smote this land with the plague of ever-increasing cold, till at last it had only two months of summer to ten of winter. Hence, the people quitted their ancient homes, Ahriman having, for fifteen successive times, thwarted the good works of Ormuzd, and having, by one device or another, rendered each new abode uninhabitable. The names of these abodes are given and some of them may be even now identified; and there can be little doubt, that they indicate a migration from the north-east towards the south and south-west, that is, from the Hindu-Kush westward to Media and Persia. The original situation of Eriene, a name of the same origin as the modern Iran (and possibly of Erin or Ireland), would, on this supposition, be to the north of the western chains of the Himalaya, a country enjoying a short summer, and great extremes of heat and cold.

Such, briefly, is the legendary story of Persia, which it is best to leave as it is. As, however, I shall have again to refer to what has been called the creed of Zoroaster, that is, the theory of the separate existence of principles of good and evil, I must give the substance of what is most usually acknowledged about him and the religious system named after him. Those who care for fuller details can consult the Zend-avesta* as first published by Anquetil Du Perron, and the various commentaries or modifications of it, suggested by the studies of M. M. Westergaard, Spiegel, Haug, Burnouf, Oppert, and others.

I do not myself doubt that Zoroaster, whether or not a king (as some have held), was truly a teacher and reformer, and, further, that his religious views represent the reaction of the mind against the mere worship of nature, tending as this does, directly, to polytheism and to the doctrine of "Emanations." It is, I think, equally evident that such views embody the highest struggle of the human intellect (unaided by Revelation) towards spiritualism, and that they are, so far, an attempt to create a religious system by the simple energies of human reason. Hence their general direction is towards a pure monothe-

* Zend-Avesta, more correctly Avesta-u-Zend, i. e. text and commentary. The fragments we now have are not older, if so old, as A. D. 226, when Ardashir I., founded the Sassanian Empire in Persia. Of the twenty-one books said to have been then collected, one only, the Vendidad (Vidæ-vadata), "the law against demons," has been preserved nearly entire. (Dr. Haug, Essays, &c., Bombay, 1862.)

ism; and, had no evil existed in the world, the theory embodying them would have remained unassailed and logically successful. On this rock, however, all the spiritual theories of early times necessarily split. Zoroaster or his disciples halted where all must halt who have not the light from on high, the one sure support of Jew and Christian alike. They could not believe that God, the good, the just, the pure, and the perfect, would have placed evil in a world he must have created good, like himself: hence, as evil is none the less ever present, they were forced to imagine a second creator, Ahriman, the author of evil, and to give him, during the present existence, equal power with that wielded by the Spirit of Good. They held, however (and this is a most important part of Zoroastrianism), that a day would come when the powers of evil would be finally annihilated, and the truth be reinstated, never again to fail. I ought to add that the modern Parsees, whether of Jezd in Persia or of Bombay, do not represent the purity of the original Zoroastrian faith, their views being essentially pantheistic, in that they substitute emanation for creation and confound the distinction of good and evil, by making both spring from one creative principle.

Of the two other great races who take their names respectively from Ham and Shem, it is enough to state here that modern philology attributes to Ham the Cushite tribes of Arabia and Ethiopia, the Egyptians, Philistines, Canaanites*, and the Berber

* I venture myself to doubt whether the Philistines and Canaan-

races of North Africa, with, probably, some of the primeval inhabitants of Southern India (the Nishadas) and the most remote peoples of Northern Europe as the Finns.

In like manner, the Shemitic population seems from the earliest period to which they can be traced back, to have occupied nearly the same abodes as in later times, viz:—the range of country from Armenia (Arphaxad) over Assyria and Babylonia, to the southern end of Arabia. That there may have been in the southern part of the same country a still earlier race, the Accadians, I do not doubt.

Certain broad characteristics have been accepted as distinguishing in a remarkable manner each of these races. Thus the so-called Hamites appear, universally, as the pioneers of *material* civilization, with a great power over some elements of knowledge, but with an equally entire absence of all elevating ideas. Their former presence is recognised in the foundations of states by brute force, and by the execution of gigantic works in stone, like Stonehenge, Carnac, &c., if, indeed, these monuments are, as has been usually maintained, attributable to so remote a period. Along, however, with this material grandeur, we find the grossest forms of nature-worship; while so remarkably have the Hamite

---

ites were the same race; certainly from what we know of them they differ greatly in character. I incline to think the Philistines the same as, or connected with, the Phœnicians and, if so, Shemites: on the other hand, the Canaanites may be Hamites; but anyhow, of a different origin.

population fallen into the background or disappeared, in comparison with the other races, that we are forcibly reminded of the prophetic words, "Cursed be Canaan (or Ham), a servant of servants shall he be unto his brethren;" and again, "Blessed be the Lord God of Shem, and Canaan shall be his servant."*

In striking contrast to the Hamites, the Japhetic peoples appear everywhere as the promoters of moral as well as of intellectual civilization. As a rule, practisers of agriculture rather than hunters, with fixed abodes in preference to tents, their several dialects (now easily traceable by comparative philology) amply confirm the early existence among them of institutions fitted to raise human beings above the "beasts that perish."

Hence we find them, in the most remote ages, planting corn and feeding on meat instead of on acorns and berries, contracting marriages by fixed and settled forms, resisting polygamy, and protecting their wives with the veneration Tacitus so much admired in the German tribes of his day. To them, also, is due the institution of the Family and of a Religion, at first, as shown by the Vedic hymns, a pure Theism—the worship of one God,—though with an early and natural tendency to "emanations" and their ultimate result, Polytheism. One of the hymns of the Rig-veda (according to Professor Max Muller) explains with singular clearness the progress of this change, in the words, "The wise men give

* Gen. ix. 25, 26.

many names to the Being who is One." Sacrifices to please or propitiate the powers thus separately deified, were the natural but later developments of the Polytheistic idea.

The characteristics of the third or great Shemite* race, stand out in equally bold relief against the dark background of material Hamitism, though, like the other early races, they too, at times, exhibited abundant and luxuriant forms of idolatry. In these, generally, we find a moral and spiritual eminence superior to the best which the Japhetic races have worked out, while to one of them, the Jews, we owe the guardianship of that BOOK, in which alone we find religious subjects dealt with in a language of adequate sublimity; the one volume, indeed, to which we can refer with unhesitating faith as containing, though with tantalizing brevity, all that is certain of the origin of the human race. It is satisfactory to know that, though, naturally, the tenth chapter of the book of Genesis,—the Toldoth-beni-Noah, or roll-call of the sons of Noah, in other words, of the nations,—has been discussed in innumerable volumes, has been in fact the battle-ground of believers as well as of infidels, the main outline there traced is confirmed in all essential particulars by recent Assyrian discoveries. It is quite worth the while of any scholar to look back at the interpretation given to it by the learned Bochart,

---

* It has been long the fashion to talk of the Semitic nations, languages, &c., but Shemite, Shemitic, is the correct form. Shem means "name," much like the Greek σῆμα.

two centuries and a half ago; he will, I think, be surprised to see how much of what that great Frenchman proposed so long ago, is still admitted by the more complete investigations of the comparatively new science of philology.

CHAPTER I.

Cyrus—Crœsus—War in North-east Asia—Fall of Babylon—Tomb of Cyrus—Cambyses—Pseudo-Bardes—Darius—Campaign in Scythia—Home at Susa—Inscription and Coin of Pythagoras—Burning of Sardis—Second Invasion of Europe—Mardonius and Datis—Marathon.

HAVING said so much by way of introduction, I now proceed to give some account of what we know of Persia historically (from the sixth century B. C. to the seventh century A. D.), and of the monuments still therein attesting its former grandeur. Now, first, it may be noted that there is no mention of Persia in the tenth chapter of Genesis, or in the Zendavesta, nor does this name occur on any Assyrian monument before the ninth century B. C. On the other hand, the list in this chapter places the Madai or Medes among the sons of Japhet, which, as Aryans, is their right position. The natural inference is, that those Aryan tribes who were subsequently called Persians, had not yet descended so far to the south, but were still clinging to the steeps of the Taurus. A little later, the inscriptions of Shalmaneser show that they had reached Armenia, but, as only petty chiefs are recorded, it is probable that their government had not yet crystallized into a settled monarchy. Later however, under Sennacherib, the Perso-Aryans had reached the Zagros, and, thence, their further descent by the defiles of the Bakhtyari mountains into Persis was comparatively easy and rapid, though their migrations perhaps did not cease till near the close of the great empire of Assyria. The Aryan Medes had, on the other hand, held for many years a prominent place among the Western Asiatic populations, and it is likely that the Persian tribes acknowledged the superiority of the Median monarch, much as at the present day the Khedive of Egypt acknowledges the supreme rule of the Sultan of Turkey, in other words, that the ruler of Persis was the chief feudatory of the Median empire. It must not however be forgotten, that Darius the son of Hystaspes claims for his own house, the possession of a kingdom with eight immediate predecessors, he himself being the ninth, a claim he could hardly have put forth publicly had there been at the time any doubt about it. The Median empire appears to have been established about B. C. 647, just when the adjoining nations were marshalling their forces to put an end to Nineveh, which had so long ruled them with a rod of iron; while, from this statement of Darius, it is further probable that there were tributary kings in Persis up to about the same period.

Darius himself asserts that the first king of Persia was called Achæmenes, a statement confirmed by the well-known fact that the Achæmenidæ were acknowledged as the leading family among the Persians. Indeed, as Professor Rawlinson has well remarked, in the East, an ethnic name is very often derived from that of one person, as in the case of Midianite, Moabite, from Midian and Moab. But though there can be little doubt that Persian history may be deemed historical from the time of Cambyses, the father of Cyrus, there is nothing really worth recording till we come to Cyrus himself, under whom Persia takes the place in Western Asia, erst held by the Shemitic empires of Assyria and Babylon.

How Cyrus attained to this pre-eminence has been much discussed; but we do not really want more than the notice in the Bible, which is remarkably clear and graphic: "Then I lifted up mine eyes, and saw, and, behold, there stood before the river a ram which had two horns: and the two horns were high; but one was higher than the other, and the higher came up last. I saw the ram pushing westward, and northward, and southward; so that no beasts might stand before him, neither was there any that could deliver out of his hand; but he did according to his will, and became great." * And again, "The ram which thou sawest having two horns are the kings of Media and Persia."†

It has been argued by Heeren (indeed this was the common view put forward by writers fifty years ago), that the rise of Cyrus was similar to that of many other personages in Eastern history, in fact, nothing but the successful uprising of a rude mountain tribe of nomad habits. But the history of Cyrus implies

---

* Dan. viii. 3, 4. † Ib. 20.

something more than this, for the revolution in which he was the chief actor, was obviously in some degree a religious revolt. Cyrus was, we know, a zealous adherent to the Zoroastrian faith in the unity of God; and had been brought up at a court, where Magism, or the worship of the elements, prevailed. Cyrus must have felt this yoke a galling one, alike for himself and for his countrymen, while he was doubtless stimulated to greater efforts by the weakness of the Median ruler, Astyages. It is also likely that he fled the court of the Median king from a natural disgust at the falsity and frivolity he saw around him; the wár which ensued between him and Astyages being, perhaps, at first, scarcely anticipated, the more so, that the Persians of pure blood must have been but a small minority of the whole Medo-Persian population. The conflict was indeed at first doubtful, but in the end, Astyages having been thoroughly beaten, Pasargadæ became the capital, and Zoroastrianism the established religion of the now combined Perso-Median empire.

The action of Cyrus was simply in accordance with the universal habits of a race iconoclastic in principle and in deed. Wherever the Persians carried their victorious arms, they burnt and destroyed the temples of their nature-worshipping enemies. The ruins of the temples in Egypt, at Sardis and at Athens, and of the statues on the Sacred Way of Branchidæ, attest the measure of their religious hatreds, rather than their ruthlessness as barbarians. Hence a natural bond of union between the Persians and the

Jews, as they were at that time the only nations supporting pure Theism. In aiding the restoration of the Jews, Cyrus knew he was upholding a faith with much resemblance to his own, and the same motives influenced Darius, in completing the rebuilding of the temple after it had been temporarily interrupted by the rebellion of the .Magian Pseudo-Smerdis.* Nor were the Jews forgetful of the support they had received from the Persian monarchs, as they adhered firmly to them.

On the effect produced by the substitution of Cyrus for Astyages, of a Persian for a Median, history has left no definite trace, perhaps, because such a change must have had but little effect on the bulk of the conquered people. Indeed the establishment of the Zoroastrian system would scarcely have been an offence to any but the Magian priesthood who, thereby, lost their occupation. Iconoclastic abroad, the Persians were, on the whole tolerant at home; moreover the higher classes of the Medians probably cared little what form of worship was professed at court. That the union of the two empires was soon complete is clear, from the number of native-born Medians whom Cyrus selected for his generals and chief officials.

Having united the "Medes and Persians," Cyrus at once contemplated making his empire the foremost in Asia; and for the first steps he took he had

---

* Ezra i. 5; Haggai i. 14; Ezra vi. 8, 9. Josephus, however, states that the building of the city and temple had also been stopped during the reign of Cambyses.—Ant. Jud. xi. 2.

pretext enough to satisfy the conscience of any Asiatic chieftain. Without going into details on a portion of history well known to all readers of Herodotus and Xenophon, it is enough to state here that, owing to the invasion and ultimate repression of a horde of Cimmerian nomads from the North, a war of considerable dimensions had taken place a few years before between Asia Minor and Media, in which the final struggle is said to have been stopped by the eclipse predicted by Thales. The conquests of Cyrus naturally tended to fan the flame, and so much alarmed the then chief ruler in Asia Minor, Crœsus of Lydia, that he was induced to seek the alliance of Greece, Egypt, and Babylon, though, whether with the view of attacking Cyrus or of repelling an invasion by him, is not certain. On the other hand, Cyrus acted at once, and, with the decision of an able general, closed on the Lydian king before he could receive the sought-for aid, and thus put an end, in the briefest manner, to the separate existence of the kingdom of Crœsus, who remained for more than thirty years the guest of himself and of successive Persian monarchs. Nor was this all; the conquest of the rest of Asia Minor, by the aid of his Median generals Harpagus and Mazares immediately followed, while we may believe that the proposed alliance of Crœsus with Babylon and Egypt was not forgotten when Cyrus had leisure to turn against these powers his conquering legions.

The next period of the life of Cyrus is involved in obscurity, and we know little more than that he was engaged in a series of wars, of the actual motives of which we are uninformed, with the Bactrians and other tribes of North-east Asia, which lasted for thirteen or fourteen years. As Arrian however places a Cyropolis (elsewhere called Cyreschata) on the Jaxartes, we may presume that even Sogdiana fell under the sway of Cyrus. Again, as we find traces of him to the extreme north-east, as far as the territory, believed to be that of the Sacæ, and also to the south-east and south, in Seistán (Sacastene) and Khorásán, we must suppose that, at various intervals, he overran the whole district between the Jaxartes on the north, the Indus on the east, and the Indian Ocean on the south. Perhaps too, as suggested by Professor Rawlinson, these wars really resembled the annual out-marches recorded of the kings of Assyria, rather than a sustained and continuous campaign of many years' duration.

The most remarkable event, however, of the life of Cyrus is his conquest of Babylonia, the more so that he appears here in direct connection with a portion of the Bible history, which is, I believe, accepted as true by some who doubt almost everything else. "It was not," says Professor Rawlinson, "till B.C. 539, when he was nearly sixty years of age, that the Persian monarch felt himself free to turn his attention to the great kingdom of the south;" and, though the accounts of this expedition vary, they may on the whole be harmonized without much difficulty. According to Herodotus, on his march from Ecbatana towards Babylon, Cyrus was delayed a whole summer and autumn in punishing, by the division of its stream into 360 smaller channels, the river Gyndes, in which one of the sacred white horses had been accidentally drowned; an act apparently silly, but perhaps intended, either to afford his army the opportunity of wintering in a mild climate under tents, or, what is more likely, done with the view of misleading the Babylonians as to the nature of the proposed attack.

Few details have been preserved of the actions of Cyrus after passing the Gyndes, but it is agreed that Nabonidus, the then King of Babylon, on his defeat, threw himself into the adjacent town of Borsippa, leaving his youthful son Belshazzar,* to defend the great city itself as best he could. And in this Belshazzar might have been successful, had not Cyrus drawn off the waters of the Euphrates by cutting several canals above the city, so as to make the river shallow and fordable.

The accounts of the actual taking of Babylon, in the Bible, Xenophon, and Herodotus mainly agree; nor, indeed, can we doubt that Cyrus was aware of an approaching festival in which the whole population would be engrossed, though he could hardly

* This name, slightly modified as Bil-shar-uzur, occurs on three cylinders found at " Ur of the Chaldees," by Mr. John Taylor: it is certain that he was the eldest son of Nabunit (Nabonidus in Berosus, Labynetus in Herodotus), and that he governed Babylon on his father's retirement to Borsippa. The reading by Sir Henry Rawlinson of this name is unquestionable; it has moreover been similarly read by M. Oppert on cylinders found at Abu Shahrein in Lower Chaldæa.

have expected that the gates would have been left wholly unguarded. Babylon, as we know from Herodotus, was surrounded by enormous walls and a wet ditch, while, recently, Nabonidus had lined the sides of the river with other and similar walls, the bricks of which bear his name in Cuneiform characters, moreover had also added brazen gates for a further protection.

Cyrus, then, having prepared his trenches, quietly abided his time; till, at length, when the night of the festival came round, finding the water sufficiently shallow, he entered the city through the river gates, which had been incautiously left open, and, in a brief period, carried all before him: then it was, as we are told, that messengers ran to and fro "to show the king of Babylon that his city was taken at one end." * When morning came Cyrus found himself master of the great city, and a Shemitic emperor had ceased to rule in "Babylon the glory of the Chaldees' excellency." Not long after, on the surrender of Borsippa, the old monarch Nabonidus was sent to Carmania; but whether as its viceroy we are not informed. It is fair to suppose that, though Belshazzar was but a youth, and naturally, therefore, little if at all skilled in war, he would, but for this *coup de main*, have prevented a town, in size representing a fortified territory, falling so readily to an enemy probably not better provided for a lengthened siege than were the Assyrians of old.

* Jerem. xi. 31.

The fall of Babylon led to two immediate results: viz. the transference of the ancient Shemitic idolatrous empire, to the Zoroastrian Persians, and the restoration of the Jews.* It is indeed not possible to discuss here the motives of Cyrus for this latter act ; which may well have been of a mixed kind : thus while he would naturally have been strongly interested in the only monotheistical people dwelling near him, he must as naturally have desired to secure Jewish neutrality, if not active support, in the designs he had already entertained against Egypt.† What, however, strikes one as extraordinary is, that he did not, so far as is recorded, take any steps to reduce Phœnicia, though, in a war with Egypt, the resources of that remarkable country would have told more against him than any opposition on the part of the Jews.

Of the rest of the life of Cyrus, we have no satisfactory account; but it is probable that he fell in a war with some of the tribes to the north-east of Asia, a conflict on the origin of which it is easy enough to speculate, as the wild tribes of that part of Asia, like

* I may here remark that what is known as the " Captivity of the Jews," was the combined result of two expeditions against Judæa : (1) Of that in the third year of Jehoiakim, when Nebuchadnezzar was only the deputy of his father (Dan. i. 2 ; 2 Kings xxiv. 1; 2 Chron. xxxvi. 6, 7), on which occasion, though Daniel and Jehoiakim were carried to Babylon, we do not know that Jerusalem was actually taken. This expedition is noticed by Berosus. (2) Of that in the seventh year of Nebuchadnezzar, at first led by his generals, but subsequently by the king in person (Jerem. lii. 28).

† Herod. i. 153.

other nomads, are almost always in a state of partial insurrection. Certain, however, it is, that he died B.C. 529, after a reign of twenty-nine years, while his remarkable tomb at Pasargadæ, affords some evidence that his body was recovered and carried back to the centre of his kingdom or faith. Professor Rawlinson justly remarks that "the character of Cyrus as represented to us by the Greeks, is the most favorable that we possess of any early Oriental monarch."

On the death of Cyrus a conqueror rather than an administrator, his vast domains mainly descended to his eldest son Cambyses, but Cyrus, at the same time, arranged that his second son, Bardes, or, as he is called in Greek history, Smerdis, should receive certain provinces as his patrimony; a plan, in itself sufficiently questionable, especially in an empire as yet scarcely organized, and one therefore promptly put an end to by Cambyses. Bardes, by his orders, was slain by Prexaspes, at Susa, but in a manner so secret as to lead to the remarkable impersonation we shall presently notice.

The first act of Cambyses was to attempt the carrying out of his father's schemes for the conquest of Egypt; so, to provoke a quarrel, he demanded of the weak king of Egypt his daughter as a second wife. Amasis complied with the request to the letter but not to the spirit, as, instead of his daughter, he sent another damsel, who is said herself to have revealed to Cambyses the imposition practised on him by the Egyptian monarch. This was alone a sufficient pretext for war; but four years elapsed before Cambyses was able to secure the naval aid of Tyre and Cyprus.

The Egyptians fought bravely, the more so, perhaps, that their new ruler, Psammenitus, was largely aided by Greek and Carian mercenaries; but, after a decisive battle fought near Pelusium, the overthrow, perhaps we ought rather to say the collapse, of Egypt, became complete. Psammenitus, some time after surrendering at discretion, was kindly treated by the conqueror, and, but for a subsequent conspiracy, would, like the king of the Sacæ under Cyrus, have probably been permitted to remain a tributary king, perhaps even as viceroy of Egypt under Cambyses.

Egypt once subdued, the adjacent tribes of the Libyans, with the Greeks of Barca and Cyrene, professed submission, and, had Cambyses been content with such peaceful acquisitions, his future reign might have been one of repose and prosperity. Cambyses, however, inherited something of his father's grandeur of character: to have left, therefore, Ethiopia and Carthage unsubdued, seemed to him unchivalrous. He failed, however, utterly in both of these schemes: in the case of Carthage, the Phœnicians, as yet unsubdued by Persia, refused to fight against their kindred colonies; and, in the case of Lybia, one army sent from Thebes against Ammon, perished in the desert, while another, led by the king in person, failed to force its way into Nubia. The only result was that the Persians lost heart, while the Egyptians were encouraged to resist, and that Cambyses at once saw his error and his danger. The old king of Egypt, up to this time well treated, was now seized and executed; while the native officers were apprehended and slain, and a severity adopted wholly alien to the usual habits of the Persians. The priests, as the natural leaders of the people, were everywhere exposed to needless insult and cruelty; Cambyses, it is said, setting the example by stabbing the sacred calf, believed by all Egyptians to be the incarnation of Apis. Egypt, "the basest of the nations," tamely submitted, and made no further effort for many years to shake off the iron yoke of the Persians, becoming thus, as Professor Rawlinson observes, "the obsequious slave of Persia," and obeying, as it would seem cheerfully, mandates she had not the spirit to resist.

But a new trouble was about to befall Cambyses, the first springs of which were, as has been remarked, suggested by the secret execution of his brother Bardes: though, even without this, his long absence from his capital, a fatal error in Eastern countries, would have given ample opportunities to any unquiet spirits at home. On his way homeward we are told that he was met by a herald, who announced that he had ceased to reign, and that the allegiance of Persians was now due to his brother Bardes. At first it would seem that Cambyses was himself taken in, but he soon detected the imposition, and then, with little reason, destroyed himself by his own hand: Herodotus, writing many years later, softens down this story, and makes him die of a trifling accident.

It is difficult to imagine why Cambyses committed an act at once so cowardly and so foolish; especially as he was returning to his own country at the head of an army, not in itself likely, one would think, to make common cause with the first usurper who might set up his pretensions to the empire. Nor, indeed, can we suppose that his soldiers would have been led to act thus, or wholly endorse the legends Herodotus has preserved, which represent Cambyses as a monster of tyranny; Heeren speaks to the point, where he says that we ought to be on our guard with reference to the stories related of this prince, as our information about him is mainly due to the report of his bitterest enemies, the Egyptian priests. There is, indeed, nothing, as Bishop Thirlwall has remarked, to show "that the actions ascribed to him are more extravagant than those recorded of other despots, whose minds were only disturbed by the possession of arbitrary power"—yet Mr. Grote, generally so calm and dispassionate, accepts the madness of Cambyses as an established fact.

The tale of the uprising of the Pseudo-Bardes, is but another instance of a revolution, supported if not suggested by religious motives, in so far as it was the reply on the part of the nature-worshippers to Cyrus and to his friends, the high caste followers of Zoroaster. From the superiority in numbers of the Medes to the Persians, as already pointed out, the army of Cambyses must have been largely recruited from the masses whose secret sympathies were with Magism, and the king probably knew that he could not count on them in any direct attack made on their ancient beliefs or practices. Nor can it be denied that Cambyses himself had done much, though unconsciously, to favor the sedition which led to his own suicidal act, in that on his march to Egypt he had left behind him, as the controller of the royal household, a Magian, Palizeithes, a man who, once gained to the side of a revolting faction of his own fellow-believers, would, of course, be of the greatest use to them. Add to which, the tales of the losses Cambyses had met with in Egypt, though doubtless much exaggerated, would naturally have led the Magian party to believe the game completely in their hands.

Herodotus supposed that the Pseudo-Bardes was, like the young man he personated, really named Smerdis; but we now know from the Behistán inscription that his name was Gomátes. Naturally the foolish self-murder of Cambyses gave renewed hopes to the conspirators, and when some time had elapsed, and no discovery had been made, bolder steps were adopted, and the new reign was inaugurated by a measure sure to be popular, the remission of all the taxes for three years: then, following the usual Oriental custom, the Pseudo-Bardes married all the wives of his predecessor; at the same time, to prevent intercommunication between these ladies, giving to each one a separate establishment.

His next step was to overthrow the existing system of religion, by destroying the Zoroastrian temples and establishing Magian rites in the place of the former ceremonies; a change not unlikely to have found favor with many, probably with the majority of the mixed population; but it must at the same time be remembered that the Pseudo-Bardes was himself a Persian not a Mede, and therefore that his usurpation was not a Median revolt, as some writers like Heeren, Grote, and Niebuhr have supposed.*

But a system of complete isolation (for the Pseudo-Bardes neither left his palace, nor admitted even the highest of his nobles into it), must sooner or later have aroused the suspicion that all was not right at Court. At length, some of the leading Persians began to take counsel together, and Darius, the son of Hystaspes, was acknowledged as their leader. We have no details of what took place, except that the conspirators were successful, the impostor being slain, according to Darius's own account, in Media; Darius adds that he proceeded himself, at once, to the capital (probably) Ecbatana, with his head, and caused a general assassination of all the Magi that could be found, an event subsequently recorded by an annual festival called the "Magophonia" or "Slaughter of the Magi." In the more essential parts of this story, Herodotus agrees with Darius's own narrative on his inscription, and where he

* The usurpation of the Pseudo-Bardes checked for a while the carrying out of the decree of Cyrus for the rebuilding of the temple of Jerusalem ; and the Samaritans were able to persuade the usurper to counter-order these works, and to make " the Jews to cease, by force and power." (Ezra iv. 23).

varies from it, this variation is probably due to the uncertainty of oral testimony. Eighty years after the events, when the Greek historian wrote, there would have been but few persons able to correctly interpret the Cuneiform records; while we do not know that he was ever himself in Persia, or saw any of the monuments himself. It has been supposed that after the Magophonia, the principal chieftains who had joined with Darius, remained about the throne, and that thus a sort of hereditary nobility grew up, the king being no longer the sole fountain or dispenser of honor. But this, I fancy, is rather a Western interpretation of a course of action, by no means uncommon in Oriental history.

Darius ascended the throne on January 1, B. C. 521, at first, as it would seem, with little opposition from the provinces immediately around him, but this period of repose was of brief duration, and he soon encountered a series of formidable rebellions in many parts of his extensive dominions, and was in fact occupied fully six years in gradually stamping out their ashes. Some of these, though not all, were doubtless connected with the overthrow of Magism; but those of the greatest importance, such as the first revolt of Babylon, and those of Assyria and Egypt, had probably little or nothing to do with religious matters. In most cases, personation was the ordinary practice, the rebel asserting that he was the son, grandson, or lineal descendant of some previously famous monarch. Against the Babylonians Darius marched in person, and, after two great battles, captured the city of Babylon; in most other cases, he was content to send one or other of the six chiefs, as Hydarnes and Gobryas, &c. It would also appear that against the mountain tribes to the north Darius found it necessary to march himself, as, though a series of victories had been duly claimed by his generals, it is clear that these had been temporary if not nominal. In the course of this war, the Ecbatana of Upper Media (Takt-i-Suleimán) fell into his hands; while the rebellion in Parthia and Hyrcania was crushed by an advance upon Rhages. Professor Rawlinson has pointed out that, so far as there is any historical substratum to the book of Judith, the events there related belong to this period, as the story given in that apocryphal book agrees fairly with what we can gather from other sources. The Arphaxad taken prisoner at Rhages must, on this supposition, be the rebel Xathrites, and Nebuchadonosor Darius himself. The Behistán inscription, is believed to have been executed about B. C. 516-515, and, if so, must have been carved during the period of repose which followed the suppression of the first great rebellions, or in the fifth or sixth years of Darius.

Having reduced the various revolts that had so long troubled his empire, Darius divided his vast dominions into a series of local governments, called "satrapies,"* their number ranging between twenty

* This word is of Sanskrit origin, and the office was common to many of the western Asiatic kingdoms. Thus Sargon speaks of his "chief of provinces, satraps, wise men," &c., (Oppert. Hist. de

C

at their commencement and twenty-nine, as recorded on one of his latest inscriptions. The satraps were entrusted with the complete rule of their own satrapies, and with the power of life and death, but were liable to recall or removal whenever this step seemed good to the monarch. They were selected from any class at the king's pleasure; even Greeks, such as Xenocrates and Memnon being occasionally promoted to this office. In some instances, as in that of Cilicia, a native dynasty was allowed to bear rule in its own province, while Persia, or rather Persis, alone paid no tribute.

The fiscal arrangements consisted chiefly in reducing all dues to a fixed sum in money or kind, but the tribute thus exacted was in too many instances neither paid in itself, nor judiciously collected. Besides this, each province paid largely of what it was most famed for: thus Egypt supplied vast quantities of grain; Media, sheep, mules, and horses; Armenia, colts; Cilicia, white horses, &c. Some provinces, too, were much more heavily burdened with imposts than others. Thus in Persia itself, where water was generally scarce, the king claimed as his right the rivers and streamlets, and imposed heavy fines for opening the sluices required for the irrigation of the

Sargonides, p. 33.) They were, in fact, like our lord lieutenants of Ireland, governors of the Cape, New Zealand, &c. The same idea is implied in Isaiah x. 8, "Are not my princes altogether kings?" The royal title of "king of kings" denoted the chief king over a number of such rulers, each himself a king. Thus Belib and Merodach-baladan were viceroys or satraps of Babylon, under the kingdom of Assyria.

fields. One direct advantage was certainly obtained by this plan, that it enabled the chief ruler to know on what amount of revenue he could count; and, though the people at large often, doubtless, suffered from the selfish oppression of the satraps, who took care to pay themselves handsomely while they provided for the royal demands, they secured this advantage, that the central government was directly interested in supporting them against proconsular rapacity. Obviously, the wiser and gentler the rule of the satrap, the better chance for the crown to secure its demands from the actual cultivators of the soil.

The next point Darius considered was the establishment of efficient checks on the satraps themselves, and here he devised a scheme well fitted for this purpose, consisting as it did in the threefold power of the satrap, or civil governor, of the commander of the troops, and of his own secretary, the duties of each office being so arranged as to prevent the concentration of these powers in any one person. Thus neither of the two former could plan or carry out an insurrection without being outwitted by a minister, who in the province was rightly deemed to be the king's "eye" and "ear." The provinces, too, themselves were liable to the inspection of another officer, who, with an armed force, acted directly for the king in the redressing of grievances. It is hardly necessary to add that the success of such a system depended greatly on the personal vigor of the sovereign; and, hence, that it rapidly degenerated under the later Persian princes, till at length the same person often secured all the three offices himself, the satrap then becoming much the same as the Turkish pasha or the Persian bey of the present day, with powers practically unlimited. Posts, or rather a system of couriers, were also established along what was, hence, called the "royal road" from Susa to Sardis, with places for rest and change at convenient intervals. To Darius, probably, is also due the creation of the first Oriental coinage; his money, of which many specimens still exist, technically called from him "Darics," being pieces of gold and silver, weighing respectively 124 and 224 to 230 grains of pure metal, and having for their device a somewhat rude representation of an archer. Moreover we do not know of any other coins throughout the Persian empire for nearly two centuries subsequently to Darius himself. To his other great works, as his memorable inscription at Behistán, his palace at Susa, his buildings at Persepolis, and his tomb at Nakhsh-i-Rustám, we shall recur hereafter when we shall describe the principal antiquities of Persia.

After a period of peace, which may have lasted five or six years, subsequently to B.C. 516, Darius resolved to carry out two other great wars, one to the East and the other to the West. It may be inferred from the Behistán inscription that the former preceded the latter, as the name of India does not occur on it: the inducement to it may have been the reports of those who had accompanied Cyrus in his expeditions in the direction of Central Asia. In order to ascertain the nature of the Indus itself, a fleet was ordered to navigate it under the command of a certain Scylax of Caryanda, and the fact that he accomplished this remarkable feat apparently without loss, proves either that the power of Darius was well known in those remote regions, or that the inhabitants were not unwilling to accept the king of Persia as their lord paramount. Anyhow, we cannot doubt that Darius was successful in annexing to his dominions the valleys of the Indus and of its affluents, now known under the collective name of the Panjáb, together with Scinde, its outlet to the Indian Ocean, deriving thence an immense tribute and opening out a vast trade.

It has been thought by some distinguished scholars that to this trade between the East and West are due certain ancient alphabets found chiefly on the rocks in the west and south-west of India, with inscriptions on them of a date as early as 250 B.C.; and it cannot be denied that there is much probability in favor of this view, especially as the evidence of a more remote alphabet of unquestionably Indian invention is, as yet, somewhat doubtful. The characters on these inscriptions exhibit, as has been fully shown by James Prinsep and Prof. A. Weber, a striking resemblance to the earliest Phœnician alphabet, and may naturally have been adopted from the necessities of a trade which, from the time of Solomon, and, possibly, still earlier than he, was carried on along the shores of the Indian Ocean, from the mouths of the Indus to the Gulf of Akaba.

Of Darius's next expedition, that against Thrace, we have ample details, the whole narrative indicating a well-considered scheme rather than an insane and foolish plan of mere aggression. Besides this, we may fairly suppose that Darius had clearly in his memory the Cimmerian inroad of a century before; and that he may have judged it well to ascertain for himself the real nature of the populations who supplied such hordes, and at the same time to let them see how great his power really was. Again, as we know that he had some time previously despatched one Democedes on a cruise from Sidon to Europe, and that this officer actually went as far as Crotona, we may be sure that he had thereby acquired some knowledge of the characteristics of the climate, productions, and material wealth of the Greek nations to the West. Anyhow, the expedition into Scythia, as far North, Professor Rawlinson thinks, as the fiftieth parallel, can hardly have been merely a raid. Nay, more than this, as Darius was at this time master of the whole of Asia Minor, it may have seemed to him a wise policy to annex to his dominions a tract of land in Europe, on which side his empire was peculiarly vulnerable. His careful precautions are further shown, by his despatching Ariaramnes, the satrap of Cappadocia, across the Black Sea with a small fleet, to examine the Scythian coasts, a commission he so successfully performed that even the brother of the Scythian king was carried off, and much valuable information obtained.

Darius then, with the aid of the Asiatic Greeks,

having collected a fleet of 600 ships and a vast army composed of all or most of the nations tributary to him, crossed the Bosphorus on a bridge constructed for him by a Greek, passed along the line of the Little, and crossed the Great Balkan, and conquered the Getæ, who lived between that range and the Danube. Arrived at this great river, Darius crossed it by means of a bridge of boats, also built for him by the Greeks, and advanced into Scythia, leaving the defence of the bridge to his faithful Greeks. How far northward he actually penetrated is hard to say, but Herodotus tells us that he burnt the staple of Gelonus, a place Professor Rawlinson supposes to be near Voronej. Thence he fell back on his bridge, re-crossed the Danube and the Dardanelles, and returned to Sardis, leaving his general Megabyzus to complete the subjugation of Thrace itself. During the execution of this duty, Megabyzus compelled Alexander, the son of Amyntas, king of Macedon, to pay tribute, under the usual Persian symbols of earth and water; and the principal of the Greek cities in the neighborhood, Byzantium, Chalcedon, &c., were subsequently reduced about B.C. 505 by Otanes, the successor in this command to Megabyzus. From Sardis, Darius retired to Susa, where he built a great palace, the ruins of which have been recently explored by Mr. Loftus.

It is, perhaps, as well to notice here two curious matters in connection with Susa; the first, that in the Koyunjik Gallery, at the British Museum, there is a ground plan or map of a town, in the centre of which is a Cuneiform inscription, reading—"City of Madaktu;" a map older by more than two cen-

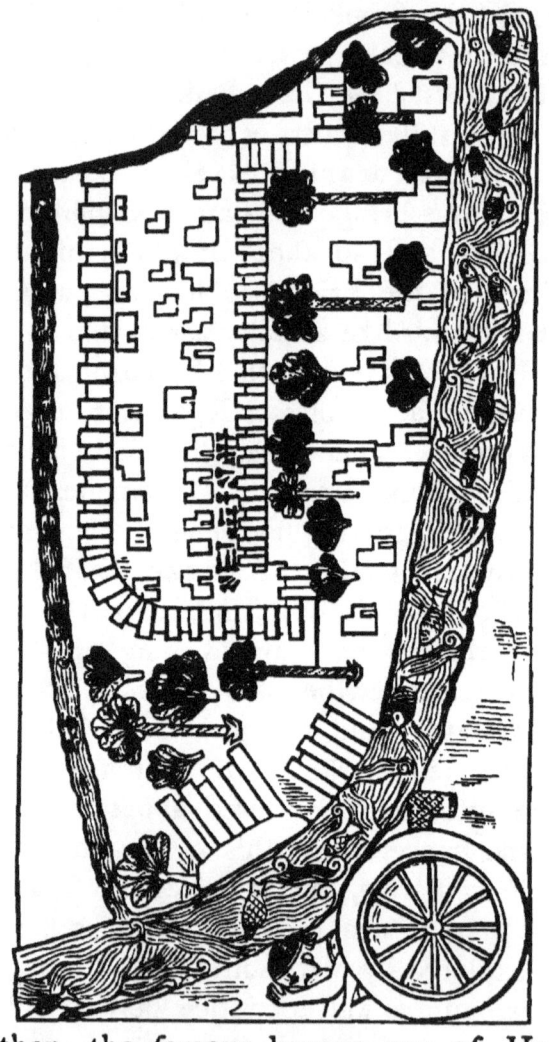

City of Madaktu.

turies than the famous bronze one of Hecatæus, which Aristagoras laid before the Spartan king Cleomenes. This curious monument represents, according to Mr. Loftus, with minute accuracy, the ground plan of the ancient capital of Susa, as laid open by his excavations. "The large mound," says he, "on the left of the sculpture, is without doubt the great mound or citadel, the smaller mound, the palace, while the town with its walls and date trees, exactly corresponds with the low eastern ruins."*

Now, although the reading of the name "Madaktu," is accepted by all Cuneiform scholars, and probably represents a place named Badaca, about twenty-five miles from Susa, I do not see how we can ignore altogether Mr. Loftus's distinct identification: I am, inclined, therefore, to think that the sculptor, himself probably an Assyrian, has, in error, engraved on it "Madaktu," instead of "Susa."

Mr. Loftus at the same time found among the ruins of Susa, a curious Greek Inscription, bearing the name of Pythagoras: the accompanying woodcut (from the paper impression, given to me by Mr. Loftus), exhibits the inscription as found, built in, topsy-turvy, and forming the base of a later column:

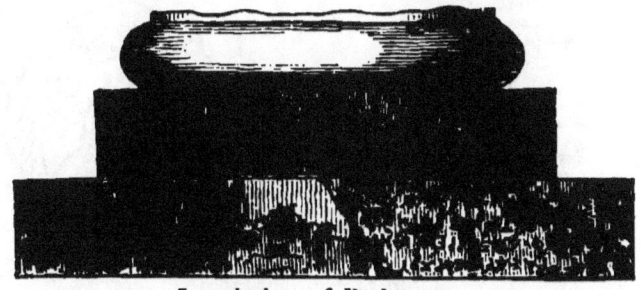

Inscription of Pythagoras.
ΠΥΘΑΓΟΡΑΣ ΑΡΙΣΤΑΡΧΟΥ
ΣΩΜΑΤΟΦΥΛΑΞ ΑΡΡΕΝΕΙΔΗΝ
ΑΡΡΕΝΕΙΔΟΥ ΤΟΝ ΣΤΡΑΤΗΓΟΝ
ΤΗΣ ΣΟΥΣΙΑΝΗΣ ΤΟΝ ΕΑΥΤΟΥ ΦΙΛΟΝ

* Chaldæa and Susiana, p. 423.

It may be translated—"Pythagoras, son of Aristarchus, captain of the body-guard; (in honor of) his friend, Arreneides, the son of Arreneides, governor of Susiana." Both these officers were, we may presume, Greeks in the service of the king of Persia; and the form of the letters on the inscription suit well with a period not long antecedent to Alexander the Great. Most remarkably, there is in the British Museum a Persian silver *daric*, with the same Greek name, Pythagoras; the only specimen of Persian money yet met with, bearing any inscription.

I have had this coin engraved here, inasmuch as it affords a good representation of the usual type of the *daric*—that is of those "Archers" of which we hear so much in Greek History, subsequently to the Retreat of the Ten Thousand, and because it is likely that this individual coin was struck to pay the Greek mercenaries whom Pythagoras commanded.

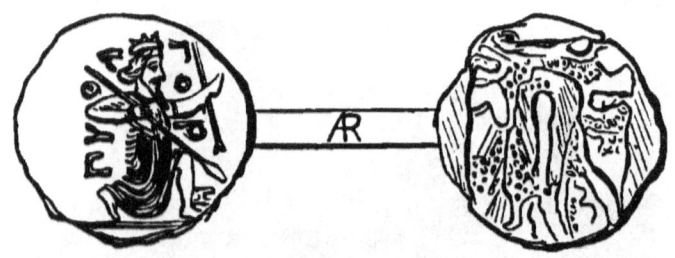

Coin of Pythagoras.

In his delightful residence at Susa Darius apparently remained for several years, nor would perhaps have undertaken any further expedition against the "Isles of the West," had he not been roused from his repose by events to which we shall now call attention.

The great Ionian revolt, which ultimately led to the two Persian invasions of Greece, really sprang out of a comparatively petty quarrel between Aristagoras of Miletus and a Persian general named Megabates; the result being a general uprising in all the Greek cities of Asia Minor against their Persian rulers, and the almost universal overthrow of the Persian authority. The first outbreak was confined to the cities of Ionia and Æolis, but as it was soon seen that they could not stand alone, help was sought from Greece, but given with a grudging hand, even by Athens, while Sparta gave none. The chief early event of the outbreak was the capture and burning of Sardis, the western capital of the great king's empire. So daring a deed could not be left unavenged: moreover the flames of rebellion soon included many places far distant from one another, and but little interested in the causes that had led to the first insurrection. Sending, therefore, an efficient force, Darius gradually reconquered each place, defeated the Ionian fleet utterly in the battle of Lade, and retook Miletus, the Greeks having to rue the day when they allowed themselves to entertain the wild schemes of Aristagoras; moreover, the character of the outbreak naturally led Darius to plan a further attack on his own part, in which he hoped to make an example of those European powers who had thought fit to help their Asiatic brethren.

For this purpose Mardonius, the son of Gobryas, and the son-in-law of Darius, was ordered to advance with a powerful force by the way of Thrace, Macedonia and Thessaly, against Eretria and Athens. On his way, by doing all he could to conciliate the Greeks of the towns themselves, and by permitting the people to establish democratic councils in the place of "tyrants," Mardonius was at first completely successful, in that he captured Thasos and its gold mines, and reduced Macedonia to the status of a Persian province: but here his good fortune deserted him: the elements fought on the side of the Greeks, and, on attempting to round Mount Athos, 300 of his ships and 20,000 of his men found a watery grave; more than this, he suffered further heavy loss by the night attack of the Thracian tribe of the Brigæ, the result being his retreat into Asia Minor dispirited at his losses. But Darius himself was not so easily cast down; a fresh army under Datis was collected, and a direct descent was made two years afterwards upon Eretria and Attica. The glorious victory of *Marathon* was the reply of the Greeks, under Miltiades, to this second attack upon their liberties. The loss Darius suffered in the failure of these two great invasions must have been very severe even to a king, at that time, of almost unlimited resources; but he was not, apparently, appalled by these misfortunes. A third invasion was planned, and simultaneously with it, one against Egypt, to be led in person by Darius, but, before all the preparations could be completed, he himself was dead.

Darius died B.C. 486, after a reign of thirty-five years, and was immediately succeeded by Xerxes, his son by Atossa.

The position of Persia when Darius died is the best evidence of administrative abilities, which have been rather unduly estimated by some writers of eminence. It is clear that if Cyrus deserves the title of the actual founder of the empire, in that he was the first to conquer a large portion of the territory his successors ruled, Darius more, that he welded it into a consistent and well-working machine, which, indeed, it was no fault of Cyrus that he had been compelled to leave in the rough. Though as a warrior unquestionably inferior to Cyrus, and in other respects scarcely so grand a character, Darius deserves, as Professor Rawlinson has remarked, "the credit of energy, vigor, foresight, and judicious management in his military expeditions, of promptness in resolving, and ability in executing, of discrimination in the selection of his generals, and of a power of combination not often found in Oriental commanders."

CHAPTER II.

Xerxes—Canal of Athos—Thermopylæ—Salamis—Artaxerxes I.
—Darius II.—Artaxerxes II.—Cyrus the Younger—Artaxerxes
III. (Ochus)—Darius III.—Alexander—Graneikus—Issus—Visit
to Jerusalem—Arbela.

XERXES,* who succeeded to the throne of Darius
B.C. 486, was not his eldest son; he was, however,
the son born to him while actually king, and further,
by his mother, Atossa, the lineal descendant of Cyrus. As a man of easy temper and luxurious habits,
he was at first disinclined to take up the two wars
his father had bequeathed to him; and would have
preferred limiting himself to the re-subjugation of
Egypt. Such a plan was not, however, agreeable to
the young nobles about him, still less to Mardonius,
who was naturally anxious to retrieve his past ill-luck.
Add to which, there were Greek traitors at his Court,
to spur him on, careless what misery they caused
their own country, so only their own base revenges
were gratified. Thus the Peisistratidæ sought reinstatement at Athens, and Demaratus at Sparta; the
general effect being, that Xerxes was led to suppose
he had actually a party in Greece who would support

* As Ahasuerus is the natural Hebrew form of the Persian
Khshayarsha, it is probable that Xerxes is the Monarch of the
book of Esther.

him for his own sake. Before, however, he was prepared to throw his whole weight against Greece, he resolved to crush two minor revolts, one, that of the Egyptians, the other, that of the Babylonians. Both actions were quickly executed. Supple Egypt had to groan under greatly increased burdens, and Babylon to mourn the ruin of the great temple of Nebuchadnezzar and of many other of her most precious shrines.

Four years altogether were spent in prodigious preparations, apparently not without much judgment and foresight; thus it was resolved to throw a solid bridge across the Hellespont, and to cut through the promontory of Mount Athos. It will be recollected that it was at one time the fashion to doubt (as did Juvenal, perhaps only because it suited his theme at the time he was writing) the truth of the cutting a ship-canal through the narrow neck which connects Athos with the mainland: but this matter has been completely set at rest by the recent careful surveys of Captain Spratt, R. N., who states that the canal is about 2500 yards long, and still, occasionally, in some places full of water. The modern name of the peninsula, Provlaka, in fact, confirms the general evidence for the truth of the story, as this name is evidently from προαύλαξ, "*in front of the furrow or canal.*" That the sea was an enemy with which Persian ships could not as yet satisfactorily cope, is no less clear from the losses Xerxes sustained, in spite of his canal, along the opposite coast of Magnesia in Asia Minor. Nor, indeed, need either the canal or the bridge be cited, as they have been sometimes, as though they were instances of mere vain-glory; on the contrary, both were certainly suggested by previously acquired experience. The bridge must have been of great strength to allow of such a host passing over it in seven days; indeed, Æschylus calls it ὅδισμα, a solid road, rather than a bridge. The builders, however, of the mounds of Susa, would have thought little enough of either work. Nor, indeed, is there any reason for suspecting any essential error in the narrative of Herodotus, and the account he gives may be taken as substantially true: for many persons must have been alive when he wrote, only forty years after these events, who could and would have contradicted him, had his history been grossly inaccurate.

Xerxes, after passing the winter at Sardis, advanced to the Hellespont, whither he had already directed the different contingents of his vast army to converge. Though the numbers given by Herodotus doubtless exceed the reality, the actual contributions of forty-seven or forty-nine associated provinces must have produced an enormous multitude. Moreover, this estimate no doubt includes every one; not merely the fighting men, but the harem and its numerous attendants, the sutlers and camp followers. In the history of any of the great Asiatic invaders, Tîmûr, Mahmûd of Ghazna, Baber or Nadir Shah, numbers are mentioned which sound prodigious by the side of the largest European armies; and yet a million is given for the host that started on the first and most disastrous of the Crusades, and the same number were under arms to protect the peace (!) just before Napoleon's escape from Elba: as Professor Rawlinson justly observes, "figures in the mouth of an Oriental are vague and almost unmeaning—armies are never really counted." There is no such thing as a fixed and definite "strength" of a division, or of a "battalion."

It is interesting to note that each contingent of this vast armament came equipped in its national dress and arms and under its own commander; while the king himself was surrounded by a picked body of Persians, "the immortals," consisting of 10,000 foot, the best and the bravest of his own native soldiers. The army appears to have advanced in three divisions, from Sardis to the Hellespont, partly along the shore and partly inland, and to have occupied Northern Greece almost without opposition. Some minor incidents occurred on the way, such as a trial of seamanship, in which the Sidonians proved themselves the best; and some losses from thunderstorms, and from lions who, descending from the Thessalian hills, devoured some of the baggage horses. All the Greek states, with the exception of Athens and Sparta, at once succumbed, and sent messengers to Xerxes, bearing earth and water, the symbols of their submission: while the handful of brave men who resolved to resist the invasion, finding their proposed positions in the Thessalian hills could be easily turned, fell back on Thermopylæ. They, perhaps, did not reflect that the troops of

Media and Persia were many of them as much mountaineers as themselves, and that scrambling over Pelion or Ossa was child's play after what they had experienced at home.

The position of Thermopylæ was well chosen, its defenders at first feeling sure of holding it against any odds; indeed during the whole of the first day the Persians were driven back with very heavy loss. But treachery did what numbers could not accomplish. A mountain track was found, and led by a native, picked men of the Persian army were able, under the shelter of a dark night, to cross behind the Greeks, so that on the following morning they found themselves between two fires. The result could not then have been long doubtful, but to the immortal fame of one small band, Leonidas and his Spartans disdained to fly, and perished to a man. The Persian host then pressed onward, the rest of the Greek army in dismay, doubt, and irresolution, making scarcely any resistance; Phocis and Bœotia were traversed, Athens laid in ashes, and apparently all Greece was at the feet of the conqueror. Nothing remained but the ships, and, here, we might have expected them to have taken heart from the experience they had gained at Artemisium :—yet, even here it was long doubtful whether the retreating tactics of the army would not extend to the navy also.

It is impossible here to go into the details of the great events that followed and which fill so many interesting pages in the admirable histories of Thirlwall and Grote. But it ought to be recollected, that even the success of the great and glorious battle of Salamis, was far more the result of a happy accident than of a well-conceived or well-concerted plan. It is certain that the Greek leaders as a body would have preferred avoiding the conflict, and but for the artifice of Themistocles, which induced the Persians to hem them in, they would have fled, perhaps to Sicily. In fact, the commanders were still angrily disputing when a Tenian ship, which had escaped the Persians, came up and told them they had now no alternative but to cut their way through as best they could. But when the actual fight took place, the issue was not long doubtful; the small but active force of the Greeks being considerably aided by the Persian plan of placing their vessels in lines one behind the other, the immediate effect of which was that their fleet, as at Artemisium, soon became a confused mass of vessels, unable to make any separate or individual effort. Thus five hundred vessels perished miserably, the whole sea being covered with their wrecks.

Salamis was the turning point of the war and the grave of the hopes of Xerxes. This conflict over, he at once retraced his steps, but he was doomed to further disappointment, as his great bridge over the Hellespont had failed him and had been swept away by the storms. The would-be conqueror of Greece is said to have crossed doubtfully in a single vessel, where but a short time before he had led his tens of thousands. "Of all the mighty host which had gone forth from the Lydian capital in the spring, not many thousands can have re-entered it in the autumn."

But, though he had himself retired in disgrace from unconquered Greece, Xerxes would not give the game up, the more so that Mardonius still maintained that, with his 300,000 veteran troops, he must sooner or later reduce Greece to a satrapy of Persia. And, indeed, at that time, Mardonius had some ground for his hopes, as affairs in Greece were grievously out of joint. Thus the Argives had made their own petty treaty with the Persians; Sparta held aloof in sullen hesitation; while Athens alone stood undaunted. But a change soon came, the more welcome that it was scarcely expected. Pausanias, a man of ability and courage, became regent of the youthful Leonidas; a Spartan army of considerable force was collected, and in the great battle of Platæa, wherein the Greek assailants were barely one-fourth of their opponents, the victory was complete and crushing. Mardonius, it is true, was able to prevent the junction of the Athenians and Spartans, but each Greek force was separately successful, and Mardonius himself fell.

The victorious Greeks at once resolved to carry on the war effectively, and, not content with driving the Persians out of Greece, proposed even to invade Asia Minor itself. Indeed, both parties were now able to form a juster estimate of their respective strength, the Persians themselves admitting that in everything necessary to make good soldiers, the Greeks were greatly their superiors. The distance between Greece and the capital of Persia alone preserved to the Persians, for another hundred and fifty years, an empire, the fate of which was already doomed on the plains of Platæa. The immediate result of the successes of the Greeks was the loss to Persia of her European provinces, and the recovery by Macedonia, Pæonia, and Thrace, of liberties their early and tame submission to the Persians hardly entitled them to regain; and what was a greater misfortune to the great king, the decision of the conquerors to transfer the war to Asia Minor.

Thus, at once collecting their fleet, the Athenians made an attack on the Persians at Mycale, and routed utterly the remains of the fleet which had escaped from Salamis; while, soon after, Cimon, the son of Miltiades, completely destroyed at the mouth of the Eurymedon (B.C. 466) a Phœnician fleet of more than 300 vessels together with the Persian army encamped along the shore, crushing also, near Cyprus, another squadron on its way to help their brethren. It is likely that these repeated misfortunes aroused discontent in Persia, for, not long afterwards, Xerxes was murdered by two of his chief men, as some have thought at the instigation of his wife Amestris (the Vashti of Esther), who might well have been jealous of his too notorious gallantries. There is little that can be said for Xerxes, for, during a reign of twenty years, he was scarcely more than an ordinary Oriental despot, the nominal head of a Court where license of every kind existed unchecked. The intrigues of the seraglio, the bane of most Oriental dynasties, in his reign began to produce their usual results; but the decline of the Persian supremacy in Western Asia was delayed yet a little longer.

Xerxes was succeeded (B.C. 466-5) by his third son, Artaxerxes I. (Longimanus),* who was at once involved in two important wars, in both of which he was successful. In the first, B.C. 460, he crushed a revolt of the Bactrians headed by his brother Hystaspes; in the second, he reduced Inarus and Amyrtæus, who had thrown off the Persian yoke in Egypt; moreover he had the yet greater glory of humbling the pride of Athens, who had sent a considerable fleet to the aid of the Egyptians, B.C. 455.

Peace having been made between Athens and Persia, Artaxerxes had no further trouble to the end of his reign, with the exception of the revolt of Syria, in which the satrap Megabyzus showed the growing weakness of the Persian monarchy by dictating his own form of submission, and remaining afterwards on intimate terms with the monarch he had successfully defied in arms. Of the private life of Artaxerxes we know little, except that he seems to have been personally of a kind disposition. He led no expedition in person, and did little during a long reign to increase the dignity of his position or to enlarge the boundaries of his empire. The peace with Athens was perhaps necessary, but by no means creditable to the might of Persia, while his condo-

---

* Artaxerxes I. was the Monarch who sent Ezra and Nehemiah to Jerusalem.—Ezra vii. 1, Nehemiah ii. 1-8.

nation of Megabyzus's rebellion gave fatal evidence of the feeble grasp with which he held the once proud sceptre of the Achæmenidæ.

The story of his successor, known as Darius II., Nothus (B.C. 425-4), is but one continued tale of intrigues, assassinations, and rebellions; the latter generally quelled with greater or less ease, according to the amount of gold lavished by the royal treasury. Of these the two principal ones were those by his brother Arsites, and by Pissuthnes, a Lydian, both of whom had relied for whatever success they might obtain on that broken reed, bribes to Greek mercenaries. Thenceforward, indeed, Persian gold ruled the whole of the Western world; and the Persians discovered that there was one thing at least Greek patriotism could not resist. From this time, all that was required was to play off one state against the other; in other words to supply each in its turn, whether Sparta, Thebes or Athens, with an adequate amount of the precious metal. To prolong the mutual and suicidal jealousies of the different states, to help each in its turn, but to allow no one to become predominant, was the policy of the Court of Susa, and of the great satraps, Tissaphernes, and Pharnabazus. "Greek generals," says Professor Rawlinson, "commanded Persian armies; Greek captains manœuvered Persian fleets; the very rank and file of the standing army, came to be almost as much Greek as Persian." Darius Nothus, (his nickname might perhaps suggest this), was in every sense the worst of the monarchs who had as yet ascended the Persian throne.

"Contrary to his sworn word, he murdered his brothers Secydianus and Arsites, broke faith with Pissuthnes, and sanctioned the wholesale execution of the relatives of Terituchmes." During his reign, while the eunuchs of the palace rose to great power, the central authority of the state was relaxed more and more, the principal satraps being to a great extent independent, nay, often holding their fiefs as a sort of patrimony, passing on from father to son.

Nothus was succeeded by Artaxerxes II. Mnemon (B.C. 405), not, however, without an effort on the part of his mother Parysates, to substitute in his place her younger and abler son, the Cyrus the Younger of history. Her plot, however, failed, and Cyrus retired to his government of Western Asia, with the view of accomplishing, by the aid of Greek mercenaries, what he had not been able to execute by the silent dagger. He had, however, to act with much circumspection, as his brother, naturally doubting him, had sent his satrap, the crafty Tissaphernes, to watch his movements. With the view, therefore, of the better cloaking his designs, Cyrus picked a quarrel with Tissaphernes, and professed that he meant to occupy his troops with an attack either on him or on the Pisidians. Having thus thrown Tissaphernes off his guard, he urged as rapidly as possible his real plans; and with about 13,000 Greeks, and 100,000 native troops, commenced his march against his brother's capital, in spite of the alarm his Greek contingent pretended to feel, when at length they learned his real object. Indeed, for a time even Persian gold seems to have lost its wonted influence, these courageous patriots having at first proposed to disband and to leave their benefactor to his fate.

Marching, as it would seem, by the Pylæ Ciliciæ, Cyrus, in twenty-nine days from Tarsus, reached Thapsacus, at which place he at once forded the Euphrates; and thence, pushing forwards, at the rate of about fourteen miles a day, in thirty-three days more arrived within 120 miles of Babylon, without encountering any enemy. As is so often the case, want of resistance begat want of care, the march became negligent, the men piled their arms on wagons or beasts of burden, and Cyrus himself exchanged his horse for a chariot. All of a sudden, a single horseman at great speed announced the immediate presence of the Great King and of his whole army; but, as three hours elapsed before the combat of Cunaxa (B.C. 401) commenced, there was time enough, had Cyrus known anything of military tactics, to have so disposed his army, as possibly to have changed the fortune of the day. As it was, he did little more than arrest the confusion into which his army was at first thrown by this unexpected intelligence. The battle that ensued was clearly very one-sided, as the army of Artaxerxes far outnumbered that of his brother; moreover, his cavalry was greatly in excess of those of Cyrus. On the other hand, his scythed chariots, though specially ordered to resist the Greeks, fled at their first onslaught, and in their flight, damaged their friends more than their foes. The actual battle occupied but a short time, ending as is well known, in the complete defeat and death of Cyrus, his cause having been greatly injured by the impetuosity of the Greeks, who, like the Highlanders of 1745-6, rushed madly in the pursuit, unheeding what necessarily followed, the outflanking of Cyrus himself by the portion of the army under the immediate command of Artaxerxes. The two brothers (it is said) once so nearly met, that Cyrus with his javelin struck Artaxerxes from his horse.

With the death of Cyrus, the war, which was really a mere quarrel between the two brothers, came to an end. Nor, indeed, but for the celebrated retreat of the Greeks to the shores of the Black Sea, and Xenophon's account of it, would it have any special interest: combined, however, with the notorious fact that this mere handful of Greeks had, during the battle, done almost all the fighting, the story of this retreat produced effects little, at the time, anticipated, in the after history of the East and West. So far as Persia was concerned, it is true that, by the victory at Cunaxa, a dangerous rebel had been crushed; but this success was dearly won, as it substituted for the brave and energetic Cyrus, the weak and effeminate Artaxerxes; and still more so, as it made known to the Western Greeks, how easily the heart of Persia could be reached, by a small and resolute force, if well led. If the small army originally commanded by Clearchus, was able to set at nought the daily assaults of a force thirty or forty times their number, Greeks and Persians must alike have felt that the conquest of the whole Persian empire was no impossible feat of arms. It is more than probable that sober reflections on the course of this war suggested to the genius of such a man as Alexander the certainty of his ultimate success, in the great war in which, seventy years later, he engaged.

Previously to the safe return of the "Ten thousand," the Greeks fancied the district between the Black and Caspian Seas and the Persian Gulf, a single dominion united under the firm grasp of the reigning monarch of Persia. They now learnt that between Mesopotamia and Trebizond, were wild and brave tribes of mountaineers, whom Persian gold sometimes, indeed, induced to enter her service, but who accepted or rejected her offers as suited their own purposes. Through these wild tribes (well represented even at this day by the dwellers in the mountain gorges of Kúrdistán), the "Retreat" was one continuous battle; yet, on their review at *Cerasus* whence Lucullus, B.C. 74, sent the first *cherries* to Rome, their little army had not lost, from all causes, one-fourth of the number who had faced the Persian myriads on the afternoon of Cunaxa.

The forty-six years' reign of Artaxerxes is chiefly memorable for the suicidal struggles between the leading states of Greece, for the submission of them all in turn to the influence of Persian gold, and for their general acceptance of the Great King as the arbiter in their quarrels. The same period is illustrated by the wars with Egypt, Cyprus, and the mountaineers of the Taurus, and for the rise of many men of distinguished abilities and little character, such as Agesilaus, Conon, Chabrias, and Iphicrates. These men it is difficult to estimate more highly than as brilliant partizan leaders, their patriotism being as accidental as the terms on which they fought for republic or king. The immediate consequence of Cunaxa, was first a war between Persia and Sparta, chiefly on the ground that that republic had supplied Cyrus the Younger with his best troops; and secondly, a six years' struggle between the Greeks and the satraps of Lydia and Phrygia (B.C. 399–394), in which Agesilaus proved himself the foremost man of his time, alike as a general and as a diplomatist. Indeed, had he been able to retain his command a little longer, it is probable that he would have cleared all Asia Minor of Persians. Here, however, Persian gold turned the balance (thirty thousand "archers," *i. e.* darics, were, as he said, his real foes), and Argos, Athens, Thebes, and Corinth, gladly accepted bribes to join in a common league against Sparta. Then we find the Athenian Conon in alliance with Pharnabazus, recovering for Athens her lost naval supremacy, and *proh! pudor*, a Persian fleet in Greek waters, in alliance with Athens! nay, as if this were not enough, the actual rebuilding of her Long Walls by the aid of Persian money! The reply of Sparta was a fresh negotiation with the Great King, ending in the so-called "Peace of Antalkidas" (B.C. 387), a fact truly characterized by Professor Rawlinson, as "a mandate from the Court of Susa, to which obedience was required." The advantage to Persia was, that the Greeks were, for the time, interdicted from getting up provincial insurrections, while she herself crushed the Cypriotes, who had risen under Evagoras (B.C. 380). This peace further enabled Artaxerxes to attack the Cadusii, and to avail himself of Athenian soldiers under Iphicrates, for a fresh descent upon Egypt. Yet neither the Cadusian, nor the Egyptian war produced any laurels for the Persians, the more so, that in the latter case, the Greek and Persian generals came to loggerheads. In a subsequent revolt of the satraps of Asia Minor and Phœnicia, we find Agesilaus as general, and the Athenian Chabrias as admiral, commanding the Egyptian forces in an attack on Syria; but their success, otherwise not doubtful, was checked by disputes in Egypt.

About B.C. 360-359, Artaxerxes died, it is said at the advanced age of 94 years, and after a series of assassinations, was succeeded by Artaxerxes III. (Ochus), who, in a reign of more than twenty years, marked by deeds of singular atrocity, restored in some measure the position of Persia as a considerable military monarchy: the chronology of this period is difficult to unravel, and we have no details of the events in the early part of his reign : there is, however, no doubt that Ochus early contemplated the reduction of Egypt, which had been for many years in a state of chronic rebellion.

In all the wars of this period, we find Greeks

fighting on either, indeed, not unfrequently on both sides; thus in the reduction of Cyprus, Evagoras, the son of the celebrated Græco-Cyprian king of the same name, commanded in conjunction with the Athenian Phocion, 8000 Greek mercenaries, for the enslavement of his own island and people. In the first attack on Egypt, Artaxerxes was utterly defeated by the king Nectanebo, aided by Diophantus of Athens and Lamius of Sparta; the natural result being that Cyprus and Phœnicia both took up arms against him and shortly after declared their independence. Not long afterwards, however, Idrieus the Carian and Evagoras reduced Cyprus, while the Rhodian Mentor, whom Nectanebo had sent to the help of the king of Sidon, drove the Persians out of Syria, though but for a brief time.

Ochus soon after advanced against Sidon, with a large army, and having butchered 600 of the inhabitants, who came out to make terms with him, approached the city, with the intention of investing it. It is said that the Sidonians, perceiving further resistance hopeless, then retired each to his own house, and setting it on fire, left nothing but its ashes for the Persian invaders: these, however, fetched a considerable sum, the purchasers hoping to recover from the ruins a large quantity of gold and silver. On the destruction of Sidon, Mentor readily transferred himself and his Greek mercenaries to Artaxerxes, and took the chief command of the Greek contingents, in the second expedition of Ochus against Egypt. The chief general of the

Persians was Bagôas, an eunuch. It might have been supposed that as Nectanebo had the advantage of a country intersected with canals, with many strongholds, held by nearly 20,000 more Greeks, he would have made a prolonged resistance. Without, however, making one firm stand anywhere, he fell back on Memphis, leaving his garrisons, half Greek and half Egyptian, to be cajoled or slaughtered, as happened to suit the Persians; nay more, on the approach of Ochus to Memphis, he fled precipitately southwards into Ethiopia. Ochus then re-enacted the scenes attributed to Cambyses; but with a bloodthirstiness and cruelty his own, and having completely crushed out the last seeds of rebellion, returned to Susa, with an enormous booty. Bagôas remained till the death of Ochus the chief administrator of the internal affairs of the empire; while Mentor, on the other hand, received and secured the complete command of the Asiatic sea-board. Hence the last years of the reign of Ochus were peaceful and prosperous.

Only one other event in the life of the successor of Ochus (who was poisoned by Bagôas in B.C. 338) is noteworthy, viz., the intervention on the part of Persia with the affairs on the mainland of Greece, which may, in some degree, have led to the action of Alexander a few years later. In this it would seem that the Persians aided the people of Perinthus so effectually, that Philip was compelled to raise its siege.

On the murder of Ochus, his son Arses for a brief

period occupied the throne; but when Bagôas found he had some idea of ruling for himself, he put him and all his children to the sword, raising to the throne his personal friend, Darius Codomannus, the last native monarch of the Achæmenian dynasty. Of the previous history of this Darius little is known, and there is some doubt even whether he was of the blood-royal. But I may remark, as a curious coincidence, that Alexander the Great and the last Darius came to their respective thrones nearly at the same time (B.C. 336); the latter having been proclaimed only a few weeks earlier; but I do not think there is any evidence to connect Darius with the murder of Philip, even though Amyntas (one of the conspirators) was well received at the Persian Court, and Bagôas, had he had the chance, would probably not have been averse to such a deed.

For the great war which so soon followed, it is clear that Darius was ill-prepared; and he may have reasonably doubted its immediate commencement (though, before his death, Philip had been elected generalissimo of the Greeks), owing to the youth of Alexander. Yet observing eyes must have perceived that Alexander had shown, even in his earliest campaigns, abilities so remarkable as to offer a bright augury for his future successes. Moreover, Darius as manifestly lacked energy; for had he but put himself at the head of the disaffected populations of Greece and Asia Minor, or taken into his pay some of the different states who cursed the memory of Philip, and hated the growing ascendency of Macedonia, Alexander would have found arrayed against him a host, it would have cost him dearly in blood and treasure to have overcome. When, however, Darius did at length learn the real character of his youthful opponent, he at once bestirred himself, reinforced the satraps of Asia Minor with his best troops, and ordered extensive levies of mercenaries. To Memnon, the brother of Mentor, a man of great knowledge and ability, he gave the command of the Hellespont and rank of a satrap, at the same time providing him with an efficient force of Greek troops.

But though Memnon had at first some slight successes, the supineness and over-credulity of the satraps with whom he was associated, rendered these advantages a loss rather than a gain in that they induced the Persians to under-rate the proposed invasion of Alexander: hence, though they had a fleet at least more than twice as numerous as that of Alexander, they allowed the Macedonian king, unresisted, to advance into Mysia with 30,000 foot and from 4000 to 5000 horse. Nor was this all: contrary to the sensible advice of Mentor that they should fall back and lay waste the country in front of the Macedonians, they resolved as soon as possible to fight a pitched battle, a course obviously unwise, though it is at the same time probable that the rapidity of Alexander would have disconcerted even his sagacious plans. Having determined on fighting, the Persian leaders selected for their first battle ground the slopes on the side of the small stream

E

called Graneikus, which flows down into the Propontis, from the northern side of Mount Ida, a position judiciously chosen, and not unlike that of the Russians at the Alma.

As soon as Alexander came up, he, against the advice of Parmenio, gave immediate orders to cross the river and to attack the Persians who were in battle array on the other side, an attack which succeeded chiefly from its audacity, for Alexander's troops met with serious difficulties, the stream, though generally fordable, having here and there deep holes and gullies. The battle itself was at first hotly contested, and on the right Amyntas and Ptolemy were driven into the river by Memnon; the personal courage, however, of Alexander, restored the day in this part, while elsewhere the resistance was less stubborn. The Greek mercenaries it would seem, fought with desperation, as men who had halters round their necks, and it needed the full strength of the long spears of the Macedonian phalanx to force these gallant fellows from the positions they had taken up. The loss recorded on each side, of more than 22,000 Persians against only 115 Greeks, would seem incredible, yet historians are agreed as to this fact: we may, therefore, suppose that, as the writers of the campaigns of Alexander were themselves, for the most part, Macedonians, they only recorded the deaths of their own tribe, the "companions," or body-guard, of Alexander himself. Be this, however, as it may, the Graneikus was to the Macedonians a complete victory, and to the Persians a defeat peculiarly crushing, from the large number of officers of high rank who perished in it. It also practically threw open the whole of Western Asia Minor to the invading army, the few sieges that subsequently took place being of comparatively little importance: in fact, no other great force could be collected by Darius, till he confronted Alexander for the second time, twelve months afterwards, on the memorable ground of Issus. At Gordium, the capital of Phrygia, Alexander gave his troops, for the first time, a few months of rest; but, early in the following spring, he advanced again, having heard of the death of Memnon, which, at the same time, disconcerted the plans of Darius. Had Memnon lived, there is little doubt that Alexander would have been attacked in the rear.

Darius now resolved, against the advice of Amyntas, again to meet his foe in the open field, and to fight a second general action, with the certainty, as he believed, of arresting his further progress. It is remarkable, that, in carrying out this intention, he actually advanced to the west of Alexander's real position, by passing through an upper defile of the Cilician mountain chain; and was thus able to fall on the rear of the Greeks, and to massacre all the wounded then in hospital. His success was, however, brief, for Alexander returned at once, and the two armies met in the narrow gorge of Issus, where even the comparatively small force of Alexander could not be wholly engaged. Arrian remarks that

"God had declared himself on the Grecian side by putting it into the heart of Darius to execute such a movement"—indeed, it is clear enough that, if there was not room for the Greeks, any use Darius could make of his vast host would be practically inconsiderable. And so the event proved. Into the details of the great battle that followed I cannot enter here; suffice it, that Alexander was completely victorious, and that Darius fled from the field, leaving his wife, mother, and all his baggage, at the disposal of the conqueror. Here, as at the Graneikus, with the exception of a body of Persian horse, the Greek mercenaries alone made any real resistance to the Macedonians. The loss of the battle was mainly due to the fact, that the Macedonians were themselves unquestionably superior to the Greek levies on the king's side. Yet these men fought bravely, and, availing themselves of the broken ground, succeeded at first in throwing even the phalanx into some confusion.

But, though the conflict of Issus was a crushing victory, it did not place Persia at the feet of Alexander; there needed yet another battle in the open plains, where the Persian ruler could fully employ every arm of his forces, to show how incomparably superior a small Greek force, ably led, was to the mightiest host the East could bring together. Its real importance was, that in it Alexander conquered not only the troops of Darius, but those also of Southern Greece. Hence the implacable enmity to him of the republican parties, many of whose leaders were present. Nor, indeed, were the survivors wholly dispirited by the event. Thus Agis, king of Sparta, collected 8000 of them, and it cost Antipater a bloody battle ere he was finally victorious. Certain it is that after the battle of Issus, with the exception of his detaching Parmenio to secure the treasury at Damascus, Alexander did apparently little in the way of following up his victory; indeed, he would seem, at first sight, to have turned aside to pick up very inferior game by a march through Syria, a siege of Tyre, Joppa and Gaza, and a descent into Egypt. But the general motive of Alexander's actions cannot be mistaken. No one better than he knew the constant tactics of Persia during the previous century, or how far the judicious use of Persian gold might avail to arrest his advance: hence, he must have seen that Tyre unreduced was a thorn in his side, and, further, that the fall of Tyre would involve that of Egypt. These two places once secured, the paralyzing of his enemies in Greece was certain, dependent as they were on the aid of a Tyrian fleet. Thus, though the battle of Issus was fought in November B.C. 333, Alexander devoted fully twenty months to the reduction of Phœnicia, the sieges of Tyre and Gaza,* the occupation of Egypt and the

* It was after the siege of Gaza that Alexander paid the visit to Jerusalem about which there has been so much discussion. Yet such a journey and his acts there agree faithfully with his usual practices elsewhere. A sacrifice in the temple according to the Jewish rites was only one other form of his invariable habit of "paying the highest reverence to the gods of every nation." Alexander did not, however, for this reason, adopt Judaism, as Bona-

visit to the oasis and temple of Jupiter Ammon. The wisdom of this course is, indeed, self-evident. By depriving Persia of Phœnicia and Egypt (her only outlets to the sea), Alexander effectually stopped that communication with Greece, which had proved so beneficial to Persian and Greek alike, and had no longer to fear the intervention of the Persian "Archers," which had so often before arrested, or modified successful and victorious campaigns.

Before, however, the final close of the drama, two ineffectual proposals for peace were made by Darius to Alexander, but rejected by the haughty conqueror. If Darius would sue in person, the Greek invader declared he would be received with due respect; but the submission must be absolute, and Alexander must be recognized as king of the whole of Asia. Need we wonder that, even in his greatest extremity, the Persian king declined terms he must have felt personally humiliating? Both sides, therefore, determine to renew the conflict; and here, at least, Darius neglected nothing that could place troops of acknowledged inferiority on something like an equality with their skilled assailants. In preparing for a struggle, which he must have known would be the final one, Darius collected his troops from all, even the remotest provinces, of his empire. Twenty-five nations obeyed his call to arms, and, besides the usual cavalry, infantry, and chariots, ele-

parte is said to have adopted Islam to please the Turks or Arabs. Moreover he probably, at first, intended to chastise the Jews for their sympathies with the Persians.

phants were, it is said, for the first time in Western Asia, arrayed in the battle-field.

Alexander having wintered in Syria, set forward through the plains of Mesopotamia, and crossing the Tigris unopposed, some thirty or forty miles above Nineveh, came first into collision with Darius (in Oct. B. C. 331) near the village of Gaugamela, around which a fierce and obstinate battle was fought.* The story goes, that, on this occasion, Alexander was so near Darius that he struck to the ground his charioteer with a blow from his javelin. A report naturally spread that Darius himself had fallen; but the fact was, that the Persian monarch having left his baggage at Arbela fell back there, perhaps in the hope of renewing the battle: he was not, however, more successful here, and though the Syrian satrap, Mazæus, made a firm stand, the day was soon lost, and what remained of the Persian host hurriedly recrossed the Zab, after a loss from all accounts prodigious. The personal conduct of Darius cannot be greatly blamed, unless we accept as literally true the words of Arrian, "fearful as he was beforehand, he was the first to fly," but this is not probable; as Professor Rawlinson observes, "Arbela was not, like Issus, won by men fighting; it was the leaders' victory rather than the soldiers." Alexander's diagonal advance, thus breaking the Persian line, and the prompt occupation by some of his best

* The battle is generally named from Arbela (Erbil), which is more than 20 miles South-west from Gaugamela, where it had commenced.

cavalry and a portion of the phalanx of the space thus left open, decided the conflict. A complete rout followed, as a matter of course, and Darius fled, not as taking the initiative, because he saw the day was irretrievably lost.

The battle of Arbela closes the history of Persia as a distinct and separate empire; and one, too, not to be again revived for more than 500 years: from this time, the crown of Cyrus passed into the hands of Greek or Parthian rulers, and the native line of sovereigns, if not altogether suppressed, reigned over only the small province of Persis, as dependents first on the Greek empire of the Seleucidæ, and subsequently on that of the more oppressive and hostile Arsacidæ. The fulfilment of Daniel's prophecy was as complete as possible. "Behold, an he-goat came from the west on the face of the whole earth, and touched not the ground: and the goat had a notable horn between his eyes. And he came to the ram that had two horns, which I had seen standing before the river, and ran unto him in the fury of his power. And I saw him come close unto the ram, and he was moved with choler against him, and smote the ram, and brake his two horns: and there was no power in the ram to stand before him, but he cast him down to the ground, and stamped upon him: and there was none that could deliver the ram out of his hand."*

* Dan. viii. 5–7.

CHAPTER III.

Daniel—Darius the Mede.

BUT any account of Persia would be more than incomplete which should pass over the remarkable story of Daniel the Jew, who is more, perhaps, than any one else connected with the prophecies of profane history and of a coming Messiah. I shall, therefore, state here, but, of necessity, briefly, what is known of Daniel, taking the narrative in the Bible as *literally* true; nor shall I discuss the question, how, if *some* of his prophecies are accepted as fulfilled, the obvious meaning of others can be explained away either as the writing of a contemporary, but of an outsider, or as stories craftily made up *after* the events they refer to. The charm, indeed, of the book of Daniel is that it admits of no compromise, but must be true as a whole or false as a whole. "The dream is certain, and the interpretation thereof sure," is, to my mind, a statement as definite and as satisfactory, as our Lord's assertion that His own words are true.

The first we hear of Daniel is his statement* that (on Nebuchadnezzar's first expedition against Jerusalem) he was selected as one of the "children in whom was no blemish, but well-favored and skillful

* Dan. i. 4.

in all wisdom," to be brought up at the king's expense, and taught the learning and wisdom of the Chaldees," during a period of three years. Daniel then tells how he and they alike rejected the king's proffered nourishment of meat and wine, lest they should be defiled by eating what had been offered to idols; and yet, how, though fed only on pulse and water, at the end of ten days "their countenances appeared fairer and fatter in flesh than all the children who did eat the portion of the king's meat."* After a while, we learn that they were brought before the king, and that "in all matters of wisdom and understanding that the king inquired of them, he found them ten times better than all the magicians and astrologers that were in his realm."†

The first direct proof that God was with Daniel occurred in the second year of Nebuchadnezzar, B. C. 603. On one night we learn that the king dreamed a dream, which, on awakening, he could not recall, and when the Chaldean soothsayers failed to tell him either what it was or how it was to be interpreted, Daniel not only declared what he had dreamed, but explained the meaning of it.‡ The rage of the king against his wise men is characteristic of a man who detected at once that the soothsayers were shuffling. "I know of a certainty," he says, "that ye would gain time, because ye see that the thing is gone from me"—but, "if ye have not made known unto me the dream, there is but one decree for you; for ye have prepared lying and cor-

* Dan. i. 15.   † Dan. i. 20.   ‡ Dan. ii. 29.

rupt words to speak before me, till the time be changed."* The point is the distinct assertion of Daniel that his interpretation was not due to any personal superiority of his own over the other wise men : "As for me," says he, "this secret is not revealed to me for any wisdom that I may have more than any living, but for their sakes that shall make known the interpretation to the king, and that thou mightest know the thoughts of thy heart." † The lesson, indeed, then read to the king, is the same as that given centuries before to the builders of the tower of Babel, and, subsequently, again, to the king himself, when, not long after, he set up the great image in the plain of Dura, viz., that such works, great as they were, were but a feeble exposition of even his views of universal empire. Nebuchadnezzar's reply, "Of a truth it is that your God is a god of gods, and a lord of kings, and a revealer of secrets, seeing thou couldst reveal this secret,"‡ is the honest language of a heathen, touched, as well he might be, by the remarkable revelation he had just heard, and ready, therefore, to acknowledge Daniel's God to be the greatest god he had yet heard of.

The result to Daniel was that he was made "ruler over the whole province of Babylon, and chief of the governors over all the wise men of Babylon,"§ and, further, that he was permitted to associate with him the three young Jews, his early companions in exile, Shadrach, Meshach, and Abed-nego. Such a

* Dan. ii. 9.   † Dan. ii. 30.   ‡ Dan. ii. 47.   § Dan. ii. 48.

position was one peculiarly exposed to the envy and the hatred of the native men of rank; hence every unworthy scheme on their part to bring Daniel and his friends into disfavor with the king, who, they thought, perhaps not without some reason, had been unduly hasty in the promotion he had given to one of his slaves. The trial soon came in the form of a "burning fiery furnace,"* from which, it may be, that Daniel's exalted rank alone preserved him; the course of events being just as might have been expected, from the greatest of Oriental despots, convinced against his will, and, therefore, longing to silence, as he hoped for ever, the man who, by superhuman means, had thwarted his purpose. He would have been less than Nebuchadnezzar had he acted otherwise; and his so acting is, as far as it goes, an evidence of the truth of the whole narrative. Indeed, his first and prompt acknowledgment of the power that had chastened him, is in perfect unity with his character. The God of the whole world was still in his eyes but the "God of Shadrach, Meshach, and Abed-nego;" thus, in His favor, the decree goes forth, that whoever shall speak amiss of Him "shall be cut in pieces and their houses shall be made a dunghill, because there is no other God that can deliver after this sort."† The royal heathen could not as yet discern the whole truth; and it needed further manifestations of the Divine power, to enforce his assent to the fact, that

---

* Dan. iii. 11.   † Dan. iii. 29.

the Bel and Nebo in whom he had trusted, were but gods made by human hands.

The account of Nebuchadnezzar's next trial is told in his own words. "I, Nebuchadnezzar," says he, "was at rest in mine house, and flourishing in my palace."* And thus, in the height of his majesty, he forgot God. He dreamed, as before, a dream of a great tree, whose branches extended to heaven, but which was cut down till there was nothing left " but the stump of his roots in the earth, even with a band of iron and brass in the tender grass of the field."† Of this dream, Daniel was again the expositor, and prophesied how Nebuchadnezzar should, for a time, lose his reason, and be numbered with "the beasts that perish." "And all this," it is added, "came upon king Nebuchadnezzar. At the end of twelve months he walked in the palace of the kingdom of Babylon, and the king spake and said, 'Is not this great Babylon that I have built for the house of my kingdom, by the might of my power and for the honor of my majesty?'"‡

But the punishment of his pride was near at hand, the narrative in the Bible adding, "While the word was in the king's mouth, there fell a voice from heaven saying, O king, Nebuchadnezzar, to thee it is spoken; the kingdom is departed from thee; they shall drive thee from men, and thy dwelling shall be with the beasts of the field: they shall make thee eat grass as oxen, and seven times shall pass over thee, until thou know that the Most High ruleth in

* Dan. iv. 4. † Dan. iv. 15. ‡ Dan. iv. 28.

the kingdom of men, and giveth it to whomsoever He will."* Yet was the judgment tempered, as are all God's judgments, with mercy, the king himself stating, "At the end of the days, I, king Nebuchadnezzar, lifted up mine eyes unto heaven, and mine understanding returned unto me, and I blessed the Most High, and praised and honored Him that liveth for ever . . . . and at the same time my reason returned unto me, and for the glory of my kingdom, mine honor and brightness returned unto me . . . . and I was established in my kingdom, and excellent majesty was added unto me."†

It would have been of surpassing interest, could we, in this instance, have found a native record running parallel with the statement in the Bible; and, at one time, it was thought by M. Oppert, that he had detected an allusion to it on the great Cuneiform inscription of Nebuchadnezzar in the India Office. We fear, however, that this idea has not been confirmed, though there is a break in the general sense, and some lines not yet satisfactorily made out. The

* Dan. iv. 31.

† Dan. iv. 34. It has been supposed that Nebuchadnezzar's illness was a form of a rare disease called "lycanthropy," in which the patient retains his consciousness, but fancies himself an animal. It is said to have been first noticed by Marcellus, a Greek physician of the fourth century. Many cases have been recorded in which the inner consciousness still remains, and, with it, the power of prayer. Dr. Browne says that the "idea of personal identity is but rarely enfeebled, and never is extinguished . . . . . I have seen a man, declaring himself the Saviour or St. Paul, sign himself *James Thomson*, and attend public worship as regularly as if the notion of divinity had never entered his head."

account, therefore, in Daniel, is at present the only record of the king's illness and recovery.

From the death of Nebuchadnezzar, about three or four years after his recovery, we hear no more of Daniel for twenty-three years; but Jeremiah's prophecies (histories?) fill up the intervening time, and confirm what we know from other sources, of the descent of the kingly rule to Nebuchadnezzar's immediate descendants.*

In his fifth chapter Daniel passes on at once to Belshazzar, and to the memorable night during which the army of Cyrus silently entered Babylon through the unguarded river-gates. Of himself, he simply adds, "This Daniel prospered in the reign of Darius, and in the reign of Cyrus the Persian;"† in other words, he survived the whole seventy years of the captivity, while we know further also from himself, that after "Darius the Mede" became governor of Babylon, he was at Shushan (Susa), doing "the king's business,"‡ perhaps employed by him on the great division of the empire into 120 satrapies, and thereby in his old age, again incurring the bitter enmity of the "princes of the empire," followed by

* Jerem. xxvii. 7; 2 Chron. xxxvi. 20.
† Dan. vi. 28.
‡ The visit to Susa is dated by Daniel "in the third year of Belshazzar," that is, at the end of the third unfinished year, a mode of reference not uncommon. The so-called tomb of Daniel, of which Mr. Loftus has given a drawing, below the ruins of the ancient city (though itself a mediæval structure), attests the tradition of the burial of the prophet in that neighborhood, and is still the yearly resort of hundreds of Jewish pilgrims.

their attempt at his destruction in the den of lions. In bringing to a close this short notice of Daniel, I think it may be useful to give a list of his visions, dreams, and prophecies, with the interpretation of them usually accepted; this list, however, is intended to be perfectly general, with no reference to any of the special theories of prophecy, upheld or rejected by such writers as Maitland, Faber, or Elliott.

Thus:—

1. In the second year of Nebuchadnezzar,* B.C. 603: The explanation of the royal dream of the image represented the *Four Great Monarchies.*

    a. The golden head—the Assyrio-Babylonian empire.

    b. The silver breast and arms—the Medo-Persian empire.

    c. The brazen belly and thighs—the Macedonian rule in Asia, Egypt, and Syria.

    d. The legs of iron, and ten toes of iron and clay—the power of Rome, a mixture of strength and weakness.

    e. The stone cut without hands out of the living rock, which destroyed the image—the spiritual kingdom of our Saviour.

2. In the reign of Nebuchadnezzar, but of uncertain date:—The interpretation of the king's second dream, and its assertion that he will lose for a time, but afterwards recover, his reason.†

3. In the first year of Belshazzar, B.C. 540:‡—

---

* Dan. xi. 32.   † Dan. iv. 25.   ‡ Dan. vii. 2.

The dream of the four beasts (generally held to represent four empires), with the judgment of the "Ancient of Days" on the fourth beast, and the announcement of the coming kingdom of "the Son of man." Like much of The Revelation of St. John, a portion of this prophecy may be as yet unfulfilled : we have, however, only to wait in patience, and it will doubtless some day be as clear to us as the fifty-third chapter of Isaiah.

4. In the third year of Belshazzar, and, therefore, probably soon *after* the fall of Babylon, in B.C. 538 :*—A vision at Shushan, in which Daniel witnesses a combat between a *ram* and a *he-goat* (the *admitted* symbols of the Medo-Persian and Macedonian empires). The ram has two horns, of which the higher "came up last."†—Alexander is clearly the "notable" horn of the he-goat, and the four chief kingdoms of his successors are indicated by the four horns which follow it.

5. In the first year of Darius the Mede, B.C. 538–7 : A vision is seen by Daniel, but we do not know where: it is, however, of special interest, as he states, that having studied Jeremiah's prophecy of

---

* Dan. viii. 3.

† Just such a he-goat may be seen on the sculptures at Persepolis with one "notable" horn between his eyes. I may further remark that in the third or Greek kingdom, the "little horn" comes from one of the four-fold divisions of the empire, which was exactly the case with Antiochus Epiphanes ; but in the fourth, or Roman empire, the "little horn came up among them" (ch. vii. 9), and destroyed three of them. A difference so striking in the symbol, implies a corresponding difference in the thing typified.

F

the endurance of the Captivity for seventy years, "he set himself to seek God by fasting and prayer,"* obtaining from God a direct answer to his supplications through the angel Gabriel † (or man of God), who announced the immediate commencement of the period, the fulfilment of which the same angel afterwards declared to Zacharias. This is the famous " prophecy of the seventy weeks " (or 490 years), to elapse from the re-building of the temple at Jerusalem, to the completion of our Saviour's mission on earth. Supposing the commencing date to be (as suggested by Dr. W. Smith), that of the *"final and effectual* edict of Artaxerxes Longimanus, in B.C. 457, exactly 490 years may be counted, to the death of our Saviour, in A.D. 33. The "seventy sevens" may be considered years, just as the word "Sabbath," is often used for the Sabbatical year; the whole phrase then meaning seventy cycles of Sabbatical years.‡

6. In the third year of Cyrus, B. C. 534:—A vision on the banks of the Hiddekel or Tigris, with a striking resemblance to that of St. John at Patmos.§ Much of it is obscure, as referring, possibly, to matters still long distant.

* Dan. ix. 2. † Dan. ix. 21.
‡ The whole of Dan. xi. (in the first year of Darius the Mede) is occupied by prophetical details, some of them of remarkable minuteness, and in chap. xii. when Daniel asks, " How long shall it be to the end of these wonders?" he is told, "But thou, O Daniel, shut up the words and seal the book even to the time of the end." And again, " Go thy way, Daniel; for the words are closed up and sealed, till the time of the end."
§ Dan. x. 4.

In bringing to an end this short notice of Daniel, I ought, perhaps, to add, that doubts have been thrown on his story, because he does not himself describe the return from the Captivity. But it does not seem to have been part of Daniel's duty to write history, but simply to record the visions he saw and the prophecies he was told to proclaim.

One of the results of the taking of Babylon by Cyrus was the appointment of a new governor of it, called by Daniel "Darius the Mede;" and as there has been much discussion as to who he really was, it is worth while to look a little closely into his history. Now Daniel, in the next verse to that in which he mentions the death of Belshazzar, says distinctly, "And Darius the Median took the kingdom, being about threescore and two years old,"* a statement apparently at variance with the prophecy of Isaiah, which, indicating Cyrus as the conqueror of Babylon, does not mention any one else, and is so far in agreement with profane history. It is, however, quite clear that Daniel understands the kingdom as given to the Medes and Persians, and where "Darius the Mede" is mentioned two or three times subsequently, this is always as a personage enjoying sovereign rank in the province of Babylonia, even if not beyond it: in one place, indeed, his title is "Darius the son of Ahasuerus, of the seed of the Medes." This is all we learn of him from the Bible.

Now I venture to think it not unlikely that this

* Dan. v. 31.

Darius is really the same person as Astyages, the old king of Media, who, as we have seen, was dethroned by Cyrus at the commencement of his victorious career; and my reason for thinking so is, that, as it was the custom of Cyrus to treat the monarchs he vanquished with unusual magnanimity, there is no *à priori* reason why Astyages may not have survived the loss of his kingdom, just, as we know, was the case with Crœsus and Nabonidus. It might, too, have been good policy in Cyrus to gratify his Median subjects by making a descendant of Cyaxares (Akhasveroth) viceroy of Babylon.* On this supposition Darius would, naturally, have reigned there during the two years B.C. 538–536, during which Cyrus was completing his conquests; and further, these two years would naturally have been included in the nine assigned to Cyrus in the Babylonian annals. Again, if this were so, we can easily understand that he would have been, more than Cyrus, in constant intercourse with the Jews of the Captivity, who would naturally give him the title of king, and reckon the year of his death, B.C. 536, which was that of their own restoration, as the *first* year of Cyrus.

Again, it is certain that this Darius, whoever he was, exercised a delegated authority; for Gesenius

* Thus in the Behistán inscription, we find Frawartish, a Median, and Sitratachmes from Sagartia, claiming the throne as descendants of Cyaxares. " I am Xathrites of the race of Cyaxares." " I am king of Sagartia, of the race of Cyaxares." Beh. Inscr. col. ii. p. 5, 14.

has shown that the word translated "took," does not mean "took of himself as by force of arms," but "received from another;" while, in Dan. ix. 1, it is distinctly stated that he "was *made* king." Again, as the Darius, son of Hystaspes, in his inscription, is admitted to be an appellative name, there seems no reason why the same should not have been the case here, and the private name of "Darius the Mede," have been Astyages. Had Daniel asserted, that "Darius the Mede" reigned by his own authority, there would have been an apparent contradiction; whereas what he does tell us is only something more than either Herodotus or Xenophon happen to have recorded. Lastly, Isaiah prophesies a joint attack on Babylon: "Go up, O Elam; besiege, O Media,"* while in another place, he makes the *Medes alone* God's avengers:† moreover, Jeremiah, speaking of "an assembly of great nations from the North country,"‡ specifically names the Medes, in the words "The Lord hath raised up the spirit of the kings of the Medes."§ We should, indeed, naturally have expected that the Medes would take a prominent part in the overthrow of Babylon, while they would, according to the usual custom of the East, be under their own kings or chiefs.

Eusebius has preserved a statement (which we may take for what it is worth) from Megasthenes, to the effect that Nebuchadnezzar had himself told his people (perhaps after a dream), that "a Persian ruler will come, aided by your gods, and will bring slavery

* Isa. xxxi. † Isa. xiii. 17. ‡ Jer. l. 9. § Jer. li. 11.

upon you, whose accomplice shall be a Mede, the boast of Assyria;" and as Assyrian history shows that Babylon was often under the government of viceroys, the appointment of a Median to such an office in no way implies, as has been thought, the intervention, even for a short period, of a Median government.

Now, taking all these facts into consideration, there seems no great difficulty in accounting for a "Darius the Mede" as the ruler of Babylon, even if the proposal to consider him the same as Astyages be thought too bold.* The interpretation of the writing on the wall, wherein the Persians alone are mentioned as the conquerors, with the immediate addition that the kingdom "is given to the Medes and the Persians," seems to be a simple statement of the whole case: while it is difficult to suppose that Daniel could have been ignorant of the preceding prophecies of Isaiah and Jeremiah, or that he would have constructed a story directly at variance with the statements of the books he distinctly says he had studied.

* The chief objection to the supposition that Astyages may have been "Darius the Mede" is that he would seem to be too old. But it is quite possible that he may have been ten years older than Daniel makes him ("about" 62 years), and Cyrus more than ten years younger when he defeated Astyages than his usually *assumed* age of 40. There is, indeed, no direct evidence of the age of Cyrus; Dinon, it is true, makes him 70 years old at his death, but Herodotus implies he was younger at his overthrow of the Medes than is generally supposed.

CHAPTER IV.

Tomb of Cyrus—Inscriptions of Darius—Behistán—Ván, &c.—Inscriptions of Xerxes—Artaxerxes, &c.—Persepolis—Istakhr—Susa—Tomb of Darius, son of Hystaspes.

HAVING now given a brief outline of the history of Ancient Persia, from its earliest period to the overthrow of the Achæmenian or native kings by the conquest of Alexander, I proceed to give some account of the principal monuments of the same race and period, attesting, as these do unmistakably, the grandeur of those who constructed them. With these monuments, I shall notice the Cuneiform inscriptions connected with them, because their interpretation has thrown much light alike on the Bible and on profane history, and reconciled some difficulties that could not previously be cleared up. With this object, I take first the curious structure commonly called the "Tomb of Cyrus," the oldest certain relic of Ancient Persia, of which Mr. Morier was the first to give a full description, in which he has been followed by Sir Robert K. Porter and by Messrs. Flandin and Coste.

This remarkable building stands in the middle of the plain of Murgháb, on a site satisfactorily identified with that of Pasargadæ, the capital of Persia in the time of Cyrus, and is in form unlike any of the other royal tombs, or indeed any other known

Persian work, while it fairly resembles what Aristobulus, who was sent by Alexander to restore it, calls "a house upon a pedestal." It is, in fact, a building constructed of square blocks of white marble, enormous in size, and stands on a base of seven steps of different heights: its stone roof, with pediments at each end, gives it a striking resemblance to a Greek temple. Like a temple, too, it has no windows, but only a low narrow doorway at each end, leading into a cell, eleven feet long by seven feet high and broad, doubtless the chamber wherein Arrian says the golden coffin of Cyrus was originally placed. It had, however, been rifled before the visit of Aristobulus by Polymachus and others, a sacrilege so much resented by Alexander, that he ordered the chief perpetrator of it, though a Macedonian of high rank from Pella, to be put to death. Its present height above the ground is about thirty-six feet, and its base forms a parallelogram, forty-seven feet long by forty-three feet nine inches broad. Around this tomb, is a rectangular area, where there are still the shattered remains of several columnar shafts, portions, probably, of a colonnade or a court, which once surrounded the tomb itself.

The first person to suggest that this structure was the tomb of Cyrus, was Mr. Morier; and his suggestion has been confirmed by the discovery of a bas-relief, carved on the side of a monolithic pillar, about fifteen feet high, which stands near the tomb, and is inscribed in the three forms of Cuneiform writing, with the words, "I am Cyrus, the king, the

Achæmenian." This relief, which is extremely curious, represents a tall figure (nearly, indeed, the same height as the monolith is at present above the ground), in the form of a colossal winged man wearing an Egyptian head-dress. This figure, of which Ker Porter has given an excellent engraving, was at one time supposed to be a portrait of Cyrus: it is more probably the representation of a good genius. The same short inscription is repeated several times on other slabs in the neighborhood.

The history of the first interpretation of this inscription, as given by Prof. Heeren, is very interesting. A distinguished scholar, Dr. Grotefend, had been long trying to decipher the Cuneiform inscriptions, but had met with slender success, chiefly, no doubt, from the scarcity of materials then in Europe, with which to compare and test his conjectural alphabet. While so engaged, he met with a legend apparently in four words, and from the analogy of others he had received from Persepolis, was led to suspect the second word a name, and the third and fourth the titles of the person to whom the whole referred. A little while afterwards he obtained a copy of the French translation of Morier's travels, and there found, much to his surprise, the identical inscription with Morier's suggestion, that the place where it and other similar ones had been noticed, was no other than Pasargadæ, and that the unique building above noticed was the tomb of Cyrus.

Since then this inscription has been carefully studied by Professor Lassen and Sir H. C. Rawlinson, and the former has published an able essay on it in the journal of the German Oriental Society. There is no doubt, therefore, as to the correctness of the interpretation. Mr. Fergusson has further remarked, that the negative evidence in favor of its being Cyrus' tomb, derived from its architectural style, is no less conclusive. It is, he thinks, a building of the age of the Achæmenidæ, and, certainly, a tomb; and as everything around it belongs to Cyrus, it may fairly be presumed does this also; agreeing, moreover, as it does faithfully, with Arrian's description of the building Alexander ordered Aristobulus to restore. I will venture further to suggest that, as the building has so strong a resemblance to ordinary Greek structures, it is not impossible that what we now see is mainly the restoration of Aristobulus; though, on the supposition that it was erected by Cyrus during his lifetime, it is equally possible that he employed Greek workmen, the more so, that, after his wars in Asia Minor, Greek artists might easily have been secured for Persian edifices. I ought to add that Onesicritus and Aristus of Salamis, have preserved, in the form of a Greek hexameter, a nearly accurate translation of the inscription above noticed, thus affording a strong presumption that this legend was known beyond the boundaries of Cyrus' own dominions.*

* The following are the chief authorities on the subject of the tomb of Cyrus. Arrian, Exped. Alex. compared with Strab. xv. 3, 7. Morier's Journ. pp. 144–6. Ker Porter, i. pp. 498-500. Rich, Journey to Persepolis, pp. 239-244. Fergusson, Palaces of

We come next to the great monument of Behistán, (on some of the maps called Bisûtûn), the most valuable of all the Achæmenian remains. Behistán* is the name of a nearly perpendicular mountain near Kirmansháh, in Persia, which rises abruptly from the plain to the height of 1700 feet, and is, as Sir H. C. Rawlinson has remarked, singularly well adapted for the holy purposes of the early Persian tribes. It was known to the Greeks by the name of βαγίστανον ὄρος, and was, of course, said to have been sacred to Zeus. Sir H. C. Rawlinson further points out that the principal description in Diodorus, extracted from Ctesias, is geographically clear, though we do not now discern the sculptures, said to represent Semiramis and her hundred guards. All of importance now visible are the bas-reliefs of Darius and of the rebels he crushed, together with "nearly a thousand lines in Cuneiform characters."

That great pains were taken to ensure the per-

Nineveh and Persepolis, p. 214. Flandin and Coste, Voy. en Perse, p. 157. Texier's Mem. ii. Pl. 82. Heeren, Asiatic Nations, vol. ii. p. 350.

* The following notice of the monument at Behistán, is taken from the account published by its first interpreter, Sir Henry (then Major) Rawlinson, in the Journ. of the Royal Asiatic Society, vol. x. 1847. The portion of the translated inscriptions, quoted, is from the copy of them recently furnished by him to " Records of the Past," vol. i. pp. 111-115, 1874. A handsomely executed volume has been lately published in St. Petersburg (1872), by M. C. Kossowicz, comprising all the Perso-cuneiform inscriptions, under the title " Inscriptiones Palæo-Persicæ Achæmenidarum." To this work I am indebted for the plate forming the frontispiece of this volume, exhibiting, as it does, a new view of the rock of Behistán.

manency of the monument, is clear from its position, at more than 300 feet above the plain, with an ascent to it so steep, that the engravers must have had a scaffold erected for them. Again, the mere preparation of the surface of the rock for the inscription must have occupied months; for wherever, from the unsoundness of the stone, it was difficult to give it the necessary polish, other pieces have been inlaid, their fittings being so close, that a minute examination is required to detect this artifice. Sir H. C. Rawlinson adds, "I cannot avoid noticing a very extraordinary device which has been employed, apparently to give a finish and durability to the writing . . . . that, after the engraving of the rock had been accomplished, a coating of silicious varnish has been laid on, to give a clearness of outline to each individual letter, and to protect the surface against the action of the elements. This varnish is of infinitely greater hardness than the limestone rock beneath it. It has been washed down in many places by the trickling water for three-and-twenty centuries, and it lies in flakes upon the foot ledge, like thin layers of lava. It adheres, in other portions of the tablet, to the broken surface, and still shows, with sufficient distinctness, the forms of the characters, although the rock beneath is entirely honey-combed and destroyed."

The reliefs on the rock are still but little injured by time, and represent a row of nine persons tied by the neck like slaves, approaching another personage of more majestic stature, who treads on a prostrate body. Of these presumed captives, three wear the flowing dress of the monarch, the rest being clad in tight, short tunics. Behind the king stand two warriors, armed with the bow and spear. The general execution of the figures is inferior to that of the reliefs at Persepolis; the king and his warriors are the best, while the conquered rebels are represented as diminutive in size. The Median robe and the Persian tunic occur alternately. The whole sculpture is manifestly a triumphal memorial, for tablets with the names of the persons referred to, are placed over the monarch and the captives so that there may be no mistake. The following is a specimen of the general form of these legends. Over the head of the king himself, we read: "I am Darius the king, the king of kings, the king of Persia, the great king of the provinces, the son of Hystaspes, the grandson of Arsames, the Achæmenian. Says Darius, the king: My father was Hystaspes; of Hystaspes, the father was Arsames; of Arsames, the father was Ariyaramnes; of Ariyaramnes, the father was Teispes; of Teispes, the father was Achæmenes. Says Darius the king: On that account we are called Achæmenians. From antiquity we have descended; from antiquity those of our race have been kings. Says Darius the king: There are eight of my race who have been kings before me; I am the ninth. For a very long time (or in a double line) we have been kings. Says Darius the king: By the grace of Ormazd I am king. Ormazd has granted to me the empire. Says Darius the king: These are the countries which belong to me: by the grace of

Ormazd I have become king of them; Persia, Susiana, Babylonia, Assyria, Arabia, Egypt; those which are of the sea, (*i. e.* the islands of the Mediterranean), Sparta and Ionia, Media, Armenia, Cappadocia, Parthia, Zarangia, Aria, Chorasmia, Bactria, Sogdiana, Gandara, the Sacæ, the Sattagydes, Arachosia, and Mecia, in all twenty-three countries."

On the previous state of his empire, Darius speaks as follows: "Says Darius the king: This (is) what was done by me before I became king. He, who was named Cambyses, the son of Cyrus of our race, he was here king before me. There was of that Cambyses a brother, named Bardes; he was of the same father and mother as Cambyses: afterwards Cambyses slew this Bardes. When Cambyses slew Bardes, it was not known to the state that Bardes was killed: then Cambyses proceeded to Egypt. When Cambyses had gone to Egypt, the state became wicked; then the lie became abounding in the land, both in Persia and in Media, and in the other provinces."

Of the rebellion of the Pseudo-Bardes, or Gomátes, he adds, "Afterwards, there was a certain man, a Magian, called Gomátes. . . . To the state he thus falsely declared, I am Bardes, the son of Cyrus, the brother of Cambyses. Then the whole state became rebellious; from Cambyses it went over to him, both Persia and Media and the other provinces . . . . Says Darius the king: There was not a man, neither Persian nor Median, nor any one of our family, who could dispossess of the empire that Gomátes the

Magian. The state feared him exceedingly. He slew many people who had known the old Bardes; for that reason he slew the people, 'lest they should recognize me, that I am not Bardes, the son of Cyrus.' There was not any one bold enough to say aught against Gomátes the Magian till I arrived. Then I prayed to Ormazd; Ormazd brought help unto me. On the tenth day of the month, Bágazádish, then it was, with my faithful men (or with a few men) I slew that Gomátes, the Magian, and the chief men who were his followers. The fort, named Sictachotes, in the district of Media, named Nisæa, there I slew him; I dispossessed him of the empire .... The empire that had been wrested from our race, that I recovered; I established it in its place as in the days of old; thus I did. The temples which Gomátes the Magian had destroyed I rebuilt. I reinstituted for the state the sacred chants and (sacrifical) worship, and confided them to the families which Gomátes the Magian had deprived of those offices..... I labored that Gomátes the Magian might not supersede our family." Sir H. C. Rawlinson thinks that an attitude of extreme abjectness has been given to this figure, to mark the difference of character between the Magian usurpation, and the partial and temporary disorders in the provinces. It appears, further, that the rebels who sprang up in Persia, claiming to be the son of Cyrus, took the title of "*the king*," while the provincial impostors are merely called kings of the localities where they rebelled.

The fifth figure is curious for the nature of the claim he set up, as a descendant of the famous early monarch Cyaxares: "I am king of Sagartia, of the race of Cyaxares." The ninth is interesting from his title and dress, the legend over him, reading—"This is Sakuka, the Sacan." Sir H. C. Rawlinson remarks that this figure, has evidently been added subsequently to the execution of the original design, it being in a recess, as though this portion of the rock had at first been smoothed down for an inscription. It may be further noticed that this figure wears the high cap Herodotus tells us was the characteristic dress of the Sacæ. The whole inscription is in the three types of the Cuneiform writing.

It is singular what blunders were made by even the ablest travelers, as to the meaning of this sculptured scene before Sir H. C. Rawlinson gave to the world, for the first time, in the tenth volume of the Asiatic Journal (1847), the true meaning of the inscription. Thus, Sir R. K. Porter, in an age when every new discovery in the East was assumed to have reference to Holy Scripture, beheld in these figures, Tiglath-Pileser and ten captive tribes, combining with a somewhat fanciful interpretation a singular ignorance of Bible history, in that he assigned to the tribe of Levi, to whose representative he gave a sort of sacerdotal costume, a place among the captive tribes; while another and later traveler, Keppel, conceiving one of the figures a female, changed both scene and locality, confounded Susa with Ecbatana, and converted the whole train into Esther and her attendants, entreating the king of Persia to have mercy on her countrymen!

But although the Behistán inscription is by far the most important memorial of Darius and of the Persian state and system of his day, there are others having reference to him, at different places in Persia and Armenia. The information, however, we get from them, is by no means so full. In these inscriptions, as Sir H. C. Rawlinson has remarked, "We must be content for the most part to peruse a certain formula of invocation to Ormazd, and a certain empty parade of royal titles, recurring with a most wearisome and disappointing uniformity."

I will now briefly notice the inscriptions of Darius at Persepolis. Sir H. C. Rawlinson thinks that during the lifetime of Darius, the platform, the pillared colonnade, and one of the palaces were constructed; the other buildings being due to Xerxes, Artaxerxes, and Ochus, of whom they bear commemorative legends; while Niebuhr, on the other hand, fancied that the palace, now known to be that of Xerxes, was the most ancient edifice at Persepolis. The inferiority of execution, however, to his mind a proof of higher antiquity, is really due to a decline in the art of carving. The inscriptions on the presumed palace of Darius are unquestionably the oldest yet discovered at Persepolis, and are therefore placed first, both by Lassen and Rawlinson. Their position is over the figures of the king and of his two attendants, on the doorways of the central chamber;

G

and their value is that they afford an historical interpretation to the group below them.

On another tablet, a huge slab of stone, twenty-six feet long, and six high, occurs the following remarkable passage, showing the hatred the early Persians bore to the vice of lying.—"Says Darius the king: May Ormazd bring help to me, with the deities who guard my house; and may Ormazd protect this province from slavery, from decrepitude, from lying: let not war, nor slavery, nor decrepitude, nor lies, obtain power over this province. That I hereby commit to Ormazd, with the deities who guard my house."

The next inscriptions, if we take the chronological order suggested by Sir H. C. Rawlinson, are those engraven at the foot of the mountain of Alwand, in the immediate vicinity of the town of Hamadán (the Ecbatana of Greater Media). They are placed in two niches cut in the face of a huge block of red granite, and exhibit a Cuneiform inscription in the three different types, arranged in parallel lines; the Persian occupying the first place or that furthest to the left.

Other inscriptions referring to Darius, but of later date, have been found at Nakhsh-i-Rustám, near Persepolis: on these we find a somewhat longer list of conquered nations; and, if "the Scythians beyond the Sea" is an allusion to the famous expedition of Darius, these could not have been finished before B. C. 492. There is one of the inscriptions (the upper one in Persian) containing nearly sixty lines, in tolerable preservation. We owe to the zeal of M. Westergaard, aided by a powerful telescope, the best copy of these inscriptions, which have been translated by Sir H. C. Rawlinson and M. Lassen, and are, in sense, substantially the same as that at Alwand. Besides these, there is a short inscription of Darius, on a very beautiful cylinder, in the British Museum, one of the finest known specimens of Persian gem engraving, and on a stone found near the embouchure of the ancient canal leading from the Nile to the Red Sea.

The inscriptions of Xerxes, the son and successor of Darius, though numerous, have little of variety or interest. They are found at Alwand, at Persepolis and at Ván, and commence generally with the invocation to Ormazd, and the formal declaration of the royal name and titles adopted in the previous reign. We are not able to determine their chronological order; but with reference to the inscriptions found near Ecbatana, Sir H. C. Rawlinson observes, "that they were probably engraved on the occasion of one of the annual journeys which the monarchs respectively made between Babylon and Ecbatana, and their chief interest consists in the indication which they afford of the ancient line of communication crossing Mount Orontes. This road, it is well known, was ascribed in antiquity to the fabulous age of Semiramis,* and I was able to assure myself by

---

* We now know by the statues of Nebo in the British Museum, which are inscribed with her native name "*Sammuramit*," that Semiramis was really a queen of Nineveh during, probably, the

a minute personal inspection, that, throughout its whole extent from the Ganj-nameh to the western base of the mountains, it still preserves the most unequivocal marks of having been artificially and most laboriously constructed . . . . . . On the western ascent of Orontes the artificial road is still very clearly marked, and on the summit of the mountain the pavement is still in very tolerable preservation." As at Persepolis Xerxes added largely, as we shall see hereafter, to the unfinished works of his father, his inscriptions on that site are numerous. Of these there are two classes—one (repeated originally perhaps twenty times, and still existing in twelve copies), a reduction of his standard inscription, giving the royal titles, &c., the other, on two high pilasters in the interior of the edifice, and on the eastern and western staircases of one of the most important buildings there, which is thus satisfactorily identified as his work.

The inscriptions at Ván do not furnish us with any new facts, and the only remaining ones of Xerxes are on two vases of Egyptian alabaster, each of which however has an interest of its own. One of these originally belonged to the Count de Caylus, the other was found by Mr. Newton during his excavations on the site of the tomb of Maussollus at Halicarnassus. Each bears the royal title, "Xerxes the great king," in the three types of Cuneiform writing, together with an Egyptian royal cartouche,

eighth century B.C. These inscriptions were first deciphered by Sir H. C. Rawlinson.

containing his name expressed hieroglyphically. It is worthy of note that, long before any form of the Cuneiform writing was made out, Champollion read the name of Xerxes on the vase of the Count de Caylus. On the discovery by Sir H. C. Rawlinson of the Perso-cuneiform alphabet, the name of Xerxes was at once detected on this vase, and a valuable corroboration thus obtained of the truth of his discoveries. Indeed, this remarkable vase ought alone to have proved that the interpretation of Cuneiform was not, as Sir Cornewall Lewis maintained, a "cunningly devised fable." Mr. Newton's discovery is chiefly valuable for the place where he found it, as the question naturally arises, how came it there? My belief is that this vase was given by Xerxes to Artemisia, queen of Halicarnassus, in return for the aid in ships she had given him at the battle of Salamis. Fragments of other similar vases have been met with by Layard, Loftus and other excavators, in some cases bearing Cuneiform letters; and, as their material is Egyptian, it may be fairly presumed that a store of them was kept in the Royal treasury inscribed with the king's name and titles, to be given from time to time to those whom he wished to honor.

After the time of Xerxes, the writing of Cuneiform seems to have fallen into disuse, though it is occasionally met with up to the commencement of the Roman empire, and there are some interesting contracts, &c., on clay tablets bearing the names of more than one prince of the Seleucidæ.* The rapid

* The following is a list of all, or nearly all, the Perso-cuneiform

extension of the Greek language, and its simplicity both for writing and reading, naturally diminished the use of even the Persian Cuneiform. The last monument I shall notice is a vase in grey porphyry, preserved in the treasury of St. Mark's at Venice, bearing on it an inscription badly written and spelt, "Artaxerxes the great king." As on the two vases of Xerxes, here, also, is a cartouche with the same name written in hieroglyphics, which was long since deciphered by Sir Gardner Wilkinson.

In concluding this portion of my story, I am tempted to transcribe a few eloquent words in the Quarterly Review for 1847 (attributed to Dean Milman), shortly after the first translations by Sir Henry (then Major) Rawlinson, appeared in the Journal of the Asiatic Society of London: "The more," says the writer, "we consider the marvellous character of this discovery, the more we feel some mistrust and misgiving returning to our minds. It is no less, in the first place, than the creation of a regular alphabet of nearly forty letters, out of what appears, at first sight, confused and unmeaning lines and angles; and, secondly, the creation of a language out of the words so formed from this alphabet;

inscriptions yet found. 1. Cyrus at Murgháb. 2. Darius, son of Hystaspes at Behistán, Alwand, Susa, Persepolis, Nakhsh-Rustám (with cylinder in Brit. Mus.). 3. Xerxes at Persepolis, Alwand, Ván, and on vases of the Count of Caylus, and from Halicarnassus (in Brit. Mus.). 4. Artaxerxes I., Longimanus, on vase at Venice. 5. Darius II. at Persepolis. 6. Artaxerxes Mnemon at Susa. 7. Ochus at Persepolis. 8. On a seal, bearing the name of Arsakes, noted by Grotefend.

and yet so completely does the case appear to be made out, that we are not in the least disposed to retract or even to suspend our adhesion to Professor Lassen and Major Rawlinson. To the latter especially, an officer rather than a student by profession, almost self-instructed in some of the most important branches of knowledge requisite to the undertaking, tempted onwards, it is true, by these gradual revelations of knowledge expanding to his view, yet devoting himself with disinterested, but we trust not hereafter to be unrewarded labor, we would express in the strongest terms our grateful admiration. His indefatigable industry in the cause of science can only be appreciated justly by those who know what it is to labor for hours under the sun of Persia; for in some cases, when inscriptions are placed very high, are unapproachable by ladders, and are perhaps weatherworn or mutilated by accident, nothing less than the full effulgence of Ormazd can accurately reveal the names and deeds of his worshipers. The early travelers, as well as Porter, Rich, and all who have labored to obtain accurate transcripts of the Cuneiform inscriptions, bear testimony to the difficulties and even dangers which are incurred from this and other causes."

It would be impossible within the limits of this small volume, to give a detailed account of the language enshrined in these inscriptions; it is enough to state that abundant analogies support the belief that the ancient Persian tongue of the time of Darius, as well as that now spoken in the country, is a genuine member of the great family to which the term Indo-European has been happily applied. The most casual glance at any comparative list of words (especially of those in most common use) taken from these languages, will convince any reader of intelligence of the substantial relationship existing between them. Thus, find—

Old Persian.	Sanscrit.	Latin.	German.	English.
Brâtar	bhrâtar	frater	bruder	brother
Man (to think)	man	mens	meinen	mean.
Duvará	dvara	fores	thüre	door
Çta (to stand)	sthá	sto	stehen	stand
Mâm	mâm	me	mich	me
Mâtar	mâtar	mâter	mutter	mother
Tuvam	twam	tu	du	thou
Pad	páda	ped-em	fuss	foot

and so on. The chief characteristic of the Indo-European tongues is the possession of a number of roots, a peculiar mode of inflections, together with a constant resemblance between these inflections, and a general similarity of syntax and construction. One of these peculiarities, the form of the masculine terminations of the nominatives, applying to Persian names, was noticed by Herodotus (1.139).

As a form of writing, the Persian Cuneiform is the most recent of the three types, and a simplification of the earlier ones, each group of arrow heads in this class representing a single letter: like the Sanscrit and the Greek, it was written from left to right; no writing distinctively Median has been, I believe, yet detected. The stories of the letter sent from Harpagus to Cyrus, and of a certain Median king,

Artæus, evidence the belief that orders to and from monarchs were conveyed in writing. Again, from Scripture, we know that "Darius the Mede" signs with his own hand a document brought to him by his nobles, while, at the Persian Court, as probably elsewhere, a volume was preserved called "The book of the chronicles of the kings of Media and Persia."* There must also have been for common and private use, some form of cursive writing (perhaps in Phœnician characters), easy to write and easy to read, as, on some of the Assyrian monuments, officers may be noticed writing down lists of spoil, captives, &c., on a material evidently papyrus, parchment, or leather.

Having now said something of the personal history of early kings of Persia, and of the inscriptions enshrining the truest details about them, I shall give some account of the most important antiquities, whether buildings or tombs, belonging to the same race.

Now, of buildings, with the exception of the Tomb of Cyrus, already described, it is a remarkable fact, that scarcely a fragment is now certainly recognizable, with the exception of the great groups on the platform at Persepolis; but these are so famous, that, although they have been given fully in many modern works, not difficult of access, it is necessary for me to offer a short account. The usual modern name of these ruins is Takht-i-Jamshíd, (the structure of Jamshíd) or Chehl Minár (the

* Esth. x. 2.

Forty Pillars) : they are situated a little off the main road between Ispahán and Shiráz, on a platform chiefly artificial, overlooking a rich and well watered plain. These ruins certainly represent the remains of one or more of the chief structures of the Achæmenian monarchy, the successive work of several of its kings ; and as such, still exhibit, after a lapse of twenty-two centuries, in the judgment of the first architectural authority in England, "by far the most remarkable group of buildings now existing in this part of Asia."* All the buildings stand on one and the same platform, on various levels, but no where at a less height above the plain than twenty-two feet ; the projecting spur of the adjoining mountain having been first partially levelled, and then built up wherever requisite. All round the platform are great retaining walls, composed of vast masses of hewn stone, not of a uniform size, but of larger and smaller blocks, wedged in together, after a fashion not altogether unlike that often called Etruscan. As many of the individual stones measure forty-nine feet to fifty-five feet in length, and are from $6\frac{1}{3}$ to $9\frac{2}{3}$ feet in breadth, great mechanical skill must have been required to remove from the quarry such enormous weights, and to place them so as to present, as they do, a perfectly smooth perpendicular wall. † Taking the mean of the mea-

* Fergusson's Hand-book of Architecture, i. p. 188.

† Supposing one of the blocks fifty-five feet long and nine feet broad, and only half as thick as broad, it would, if in limestone, weigh above fifteen tons, and if in marble, considerably more

surements of those travelers who can the best be relied on, Mr. Fergusson estimates the greatest length and breadth of the platform at 1,500 and 950 feet respectively.

The outline of this remarkable platform is irregular, a fact probably due to the nature of the ground; the present level is also very uneven, owing chiefly to the vast accumulation on it of fallen ruins: to the north, the native rock shows marks of the tools by which the upper portions were hewn down; and in the adjacent quarries are still many slabs carved and ready for removal. It is clear, therefore, that here, as is the case with some of the great buildings in Egypt, additions contemplated were never carried into effect. The arrangement of the buildings on and within the boundary of the great platform, will be best understood, if it is borne in mind that they stand on three distinct terraces, each varying in some degree from the other, as regards their respective heights above the plain. Of these there still exist—that to the south; that about twenty-three feet above it; that to the north, about thirty-five feet; and, between these two, the central or upper terrace, on which repose the noblest remains, which is as much as forty-five feet.

To reach these levels from the plain, and from one to the other, there is a series of gigantic staircases, unique in character and execution, which form one of the most characteristic features of Persepolitan art. Of these the grandest is that towards the northern end of the west front, which is still the only mode of access from the plain below. This staircase consists of a vast double flight of steps, rising from the south and the north, with a very gentle ascent, the height of each step being in no instance more than four inches. Indeed the ascent is so gradual, that Sir R. K. Porter and other travelers used to ride up it on horseback. The width of the staircase is twenty-two feet, sufficient (it is said) to allow ten horsemen to ride up it abreast, the blocks used in their construction being often so vast, as to allow of ten to fourteen steps being cut out of the same block. It is a remarkable peculiarity in the construction, that the staircase does not project from the retaining wall, but is, as it were, taken out of it.

On ascending the first flight, an oblong landing-place presents itself, whence springs a second flight of forty-eight steps; while a couple of corresponding staircases form a landing-place on the grand level of the platform. Well may Fergusson exclaim that this is "the noblest example of a flight of stairs to be found in any part of the world."* Several other sets of smaller staircases occur in different parts of the platform, each one exhibiting some point of difference worthy of attention in a detailed history of the site. It is enough here to notice particularly the one ascending from the level of the northern platform to the central or upper terrace. This staircase consists of four single flights of steps, two in the centre facing each other and leading to a projecting

---

* Fergusson, Palaces of Nineveh and Persepolis, pp. 102, 103.

landing-place, and two others on either side of the central flights at a distance of about twenty-one yards. These steps are sixteen feet wide; the whole of the upright sides are covered with sculptures, whereas the great outer one from the plain is unsculptured. These sculptures consist of, first, on the spandrils, a lion devouring a bull; and secondly, in the compartment between the spandrils, eight colossal Persian guards, armed with a spear, sword or shield. Beyond the spandril, where it slopes so as to form a parapet for the steps, a row of cypress trees have been carved, and at the end of the parapet, and along the whole of the inner face, is a set of small figures, representing guards as before, but this time generally with the bow and quiver, instead of the shield. Along the extreme edge of the parapet, externally, was a narrow border thickly set with rosettes. Again, in the long spaces between the central stairs and those on either side of them, are repetitions of the lion and bull sculpture, while between them and the central stairs, the face of the wall is divided horizontally into three bands, each of which has once possessed its continuous row of figures. The principal subject, both of the right and left sides, is the bringing of tribute to the king by various subject nations. Three blank spaces have been left, probably in each case for inscriptions; in one instance only, however, has this been carried into effect, viz. on the right hand or western end of the staircase, where may be plainly read, " Xerxes the great king, the king of kings, the son of king Darius, the Achæmenian." The usual Assyrian and Scythic versions have been here omitted.* On another staircase is a tablet with the name of Ochus. Mr. Rich also noticed another staircase cut out of the solid rock, and serving as a means of communication between the southern and central terraces.

The principal buildings on the platform are five in number, four on the central or upper terrace, and one at its end towards the mountain. Three of the first class may be conveniently named from their respective founders, the "Palaces" of Darius, Xerxes, and Artaxerxes III., Ochus: the fourth, is the great pillared hall, called by Professor Rawlinson, "The Hall of Audience." To the fifth no other name can be given but that of the "Eastern Edifice." The palace of Darius was on the western, and highest part of the platform, and exhibits remains of several chambers, with external rooms, apparently guard-rooms, from the sculpture on the jambs of their door-ways of gigantic guards, armed with spears. Behind each guard-room was a principal room, fifty feet square, the roof having been originally supported by sixteen pillars, the bases of which only now remain. The only sculptures found in or near these rooms, on the jambs of the door-ways, are reliefs representing the king, followed by two attendants, one of whom holds the umbrella over his head, and the other a cloth and a fly-flapper; or, engaged in forcing back

* There would seem to be six other staircases with double flights, two of which belong to the "Palace of Darius" and two to that of "Xerxes."

and slaying a lion or some other monster, who is apparently trying to make his way into the palace. In the rear are traces of several smaller apartments.

The measurements, conducted by Messrs. Flandin and Coste on the spot, have not determined whether this building ever had an upper story, but Mr. Fergusson has inferred from the Tomb of Darius (which we shall describe presently), that the pillars must have been intended to support such a story as is there indicated. As only the bases have been found, it is likely that the pillars themselves were of wood, thin and light, perhaps of cedar, or of some other rare and valuable timber,* and doubtless richly overlaid with precious metals or brilliant colors. As in other cases, the existing remains here are probably those of "Halls of Audience," while the private apartments of the great king, "the king's house," of the Bible, were doubtless contiguous, but somewhat behind; distinct again from them, as now, in all Muhammedan countries, and in conformity with the graphic details in the story of Esther, was the "Women's House:" † for all of them, there is ample room on the great platform.

The Palace of Xerxes differs little from that of Darius, except that it is still larger, the principal hall being eighty, instead of fifty feet square, with thirty-six, instead of sixteen pillars, to carry the

---

* Polybius states this of the palace at Ecbatana (x. c. 27). In some of the recent excavations in Southern Babylonia, beams of teak have been found, which prove an early intercourse with India.

† Esth. ii. 12-14.

roof. Two of the larger of the side apartments, had also each four supporting pillars, and by setting the chief structure well back on the platform, room has been obtained for a magnificently wide terrace. In ornamentation, the combats of the king with the lions or monsters, is replaced by attendants, who bring articles for the toilette or the table, perhaps indicating as does also the architecture, the rapidly increasing growth of luxury. If, indeed, the Ahasuerus of Esther be the Xerxes of history, the general description in chapter ii., especially, and that of the great banquet given by Esther, fully corroborate what we learn elsewhere, of the luxury of the Court in those later days. The Palace of Ochus, in its leading features, would seem to have been much like that of Xerxes, but is now too ruined to be worth describing.

The fifth structure is what we have called the *Eastern Palace.* Here (if indeed Cyrus built anything) it is probable that we see his work; a smaller building on a platform, not so high as that of Darius, yet bearing a remarkable resemblance to it. No inscriptions have as yet been discovered here, nor traces of the usual accompanying chambers; but the fragments remaining are peculiarly massive, and the sculpture in very bold relief. As it faces the north, Professor Rawlinson suggests that it may have been built by Darius as a summer palace.

I have now noticed all the buildings that were intended more or less for purposes of habitation. Besides these, however, are the Propylæa, (gate-ways and guard chambers) commanding the entrances to the principal buildings, together with remains of other halls of vast size, probably once throne rooms. The former would seem to have been four in number: one of the largest, directly opposite the centre of the landing place from the plain, consisting of a great hall, eighty-two feet square, with a roof supported by four columns, each between fifty and sixty feet high; its walls were fully sixteen feet thick, and the portals (each twelve feet wide and thirty-six high), pointed respectively to the head of the stairs, or to the east. As is the case in the Assyrian palaces, both of these portals were flanked by colossal man-headed bulls, which still retain, though much injured by their long exposure to the weather and to the rapacity of man, much of their original grandeur. The remarkable preservation of many of the finest of the Assyrian monuments is due, it must be remembered, to the fortunate accident of their burial, soon after the fall of Nineveh, in the soft clay, mainly produced by the disintegration of the unburnt bricks, of which the walls they decorated were composed.

One distinguishing feature, indeed, of Persepolis is, that the walls have wholly disappeared, notwithstanding their enormous thickness; hence Mr. Fergusson has conjectured that they were made entirely of clay, which, in the lapse of centuries, would perish under the influence of the winter rains and summer suns. Professor Rawlinson, on the other hand, suggests that they may have been constructed of small

H

stones, which the natives of the neighborhood would be able and glad to carry off for their own purposes. It is not necessary to discuss here the meaning of the monsters and other mythical animals visible on Persepolitan sculptures; but I may remark, that throughout Pagan mythology, the lion and the bull are usual emblems of force and power; just as in the Bible, the horns of an animal are symbols of might and strength, of success and dominion. Thus Daniel says, "The great horn which is between his eyes, is the first king." There is also a famous passage in Ezekiel,* the imagery of which some have thought was suggested by the Ninevite monuments he might have seen while yet uncovered. Again, Alexander the Great is called in Oriental history *Zu'l-Karnain*, or "he of the two horns," in allusion, perhaps, to his claim of descent from Jupiter Ammon, perpetuated as this is also on the coins, believed to bear his portrait. Daniel also (as we have seen) foretells the establishment of his empire, under the combination of human and bestial types.†

Three other buildings remain, which have all had *Propylæa*, but they are much mutilated, and their purposes have not therefore been determined. One of these has been supposed by Sir R. K. Porter to represent the building said to have been fired by Alexander the Great; but if so, careful examination of the remaining stone-work would surely show some traces of the calcining action of intense heat. On the other hand, we should have supposed that if

* Ezek. i. 7, 9-10. † Daniel vii. 4.

Alexander did really destroy by fire any building at Persepolis, he would have chosen for this barbarism, the finest building on the platform, and not one certainly inferior to some of the others.

Of the Chehl Minár or great pillared Hall of Audience (sometimes called "The Hall of One Hundred Columns"), which we must now describe, Mr. Fergusson remarks, "We have no cathedral in England which at all comes near it in dimensions; nor indeed in France or Germany is there one that covers so much ground. Cologne comes nearest to it . . . but, of course, the comparison is hardly fair, as these buildings had stone roofs, and were far higher. But in linear horizontal dimensions, the only edifice of the Middle Ages that comes up to it, is Milan Cathedral, which covers 107,800 feet, and (taken all in all) is perhaps, the building that resembles it most in style and in the general character of the effect it must have produced on the spectator."* This great hall was approached by a portico, about 183 feet long, and fifty-two deep, its roof being sustained by sixteen pillars, thirty-five feet high, arranged in two rows of eight each. Behind this portico was the great chamber itself, a square of 227 feet, believed (from calculation, rather than from actually existing remains) to have been supported by 100 columns of the same height as those of the portico, in ten rows of ten each. The walls inclosing it were about ten-and-a-half feet thick, with two door-

* Fergusson, Palaces, pp. 171-2. Handbook of Architecture, i. p. 197.

ways at each end, exactly opposite the one to the other. In the spaces of the wall, on either side of the doorways, to the east, west, and south, were three niches, all carrying the usual square tops of the Persepolitan windows and doors. No trace remains here, as in the case of the other "halls," of any smaller buildings attached to it. All the ornamentation indicates that the building was intended for public purposes, as here the monarch is seen sitting on his throne, under a canopy, with the tiara on his head, or engaged in destroying symbolical monsters. Again, on the jambs of the great doors is the same representation of seated majesty, while below him are guards, arranged five and five; the whole number of figures represented amounting to two hundred. On the doors at the back of the building, the throne is represented as raised upon a lofty platform, the stages of which, three in number, are supported by figures differently dressed, perhaps to indicate the natives of different provinces.

"It is a reasonable conjecture," adds Professor Rawlinson, "that this great hall was intended especially for a throne-room, and that, in the representations on these doorways, we have figured a structure which actually existed under its roof." I ought to add that of the 116 pillars, once in the hall and porch, eight bases only have as yet been discovered, six in the hall, and two in the porch, but I cannot help thinking that if another Layard will do for Persepolis one-half he did for Nineveh, much more may yet be found, and many unsolved problems set at rest. In front of the portico of the "Hall of a Hundred Columns," still stand the mutilated remains of what were probably man-headed bulls, though it must be admitted, that this is not quite certain, owing to their present ruined state. The columns and the composite capitals, of this portico, are of the same character as those in the Eastern Palace, the blocks of stone being often ten feet square by seven thick; hence Professor Rawlinson infers that this room may have served as the audience chamber of its builder.

We come now to the last, but, on the whole, the greatest work on the whole platform, another great "Hall of Audience," the remains of which, stretching 350 feet in one direction, and 256 feet in the other, comprehend more than 20,000 square feet. Its existing ruins consist almost wholly of four groups of enormous pillars, of the extraordinary height of sixty-four feet, carrying capitals formed of either two half-gryphons or two half-bulls, back to back, and themselves varying considerably from plain and simple fluting, to a remarkable richness of ornamentation. The bases of the columns are of great beauty, in form bell-shaped, and adorned with a double or triple row of pendent lotus-leaves, some rounded, and some narrowed to a point. Capitals and bases perfectly resembling these, and scarcely inferior to them in beauty of execution, were found by Mr. Loftus, in his excavations at Susa. There can be little doubt that these halls were once covered with a wooden roof, the double-bull capital being admirably adapted to support the ends of the beams. Indeed the use of such capitals is perfectly evident, from the copy in stone of a timber roof observable in the famous tomb of Darius at Nakhsh-i-Rustám.

The architectural controversy, as to what the walls round this gigantic room were made of, need not be discussed; the more so as it must be confessed, that all the theories proposed involve grave difficulties. Judging from other cases, had the walls been of stone, we should expect to find some traces of them; while, on the other hand, it is hard to believe such a builder as Xerxes, with an unlimited supply of stone close at hand, would have used bricks, which were a necessity for the Assyrians and Babylonians, as for them stone had to be brought from a considerable distance. After all, the most probable description is that in Esther, evidently an account of a summer throne-room. "And when those days were expired, the king made a feast unto all the people that were present in Shushan the palace, unto great and small, seven days, in the court of the garden of the king's palace: where were white, green, and blue hangings, fastened with cords of fine linen, and purple to silver rings, and pillars of marble; the beds were of gold and silver, upon a pavement of red, blue, and white and black marble."* The heat of an ordinary Persian summer, suggests the probability of such an arrangement, indeed, Loftus, in his notice of his excavations at Susa, remarks that

* Esther i. 5–6.

"nothing could be more appropriate than this method at Susa and Persepolis, the spring residences of the Persian monarchs. It must be considered that these columnar halls were the equivalents of the modern throne-rooms; here all public business was despatched, and here the king might sit and enjoy the beauties of the landscape."*

Such must serve for some account of the far-famed Persepolis. In concluding this portion of my book, I will only say a few words on the remaining palaces known to have belonged to the Persian kings of the Achæmenian dynasty, and shall then briefly notice some of their tombs.

The other palaces are the ruins found at Murgháb, near the tomb of Cyrus; at Istakhr, on the edge of the valley leading thence to Persepolis; and at Susa. Those at Ecbatana and in the town of Persepolis have scarcely left even ruins. One of these structures at Murgháb, as bearing the well-known inscription, "I am Cyrus the king, the Achæmenian," has been reasonably supposed to have been occupied, if not built by him. This building appears to be in form an oblong, of 147 feet by 116. Within it stands a single shaft, 36 feet high, and on the paved area around, are the remains of the basis of seven similar columns. If Messrs. Flandin and Coste are right, there were three rows, each containing four pillars originally; and this number of rows corresponds, as Professor Rawlinson has remarked, to the number in Solomon's House of the Forest of Lebanon."† The

---

* Loftus, Chaldæa and Susiana, p. 375.   † 1 Kings vii. 8

smaller building, which is hard by, is a longer oblong, of 125 feet by 50. It is in front of this building that the square column stands, with the mythological relief on it, which we have already described. There is also in the immediate neighborhood, the remains of a platform of huge square stones, rusticated, after a fashion, not unlike the substructions of the temple at Jerusalem, recently brought to light by the excavations of the Palestine Fund. Mr. Rich, who has described it fully, mentions one stone fourteen feet two inches long; and Flandin and Coste more than one so enormous as thirty-two feet nine inches in length. The outline of the palace at Istakhr is well preserved, though only one column, twenty-five feet high, is standing, with the basis of eight others. The walls have been partially traced, and the jambs of several doorways detected.

The palace at Susa has been fully described, from his excavations there, by Mr. Loftus, and is evidently in form a duplicate of Darius's palace at Persepolis. It stood, however, on a platform of sundried brick, originally constructed at a very remote period, probably by some of the Kushite or Accadian rulers of Susiana. An inscription repeated on the basis of four pillars, proves that the building, resting on this mass of early brickwork, was erected originally by Darius; while another inscription confirms its reparation by Artaxerxes I. (Longimanus). It was at Susa, it will be remembered, that Daniel saw the vision of the ram with the two horns. "And I saw in a vision, and it came to pass, when I saw, that I

Tomb of Darius.

was at Shushan, in the palace, which is in the province of Elam; and I saw in a vision,"* &c.

The remaining tombs of the kings of Persia show much resemblance to the tombs in Lycia and at Petra, in so far that they are formed by excavations on the sides of the hills, generally at a considerable height above the ground. Of this peculiar class of tombs there appear to be seven; four in the valley of the Pulwar, to the northwest, and three near to Persepolis itself. They are all on the same plan, consisting generally of an upper space, in which the king is represented worshiping Ormazd; and under this what might be a portico, but that the four columns are all engaged;—that is, are really pilasters carved on the face of the rock, into the similitude of pillars. In the middle is an apparent door way, though the actual entrance into the tomb is below and behind the ornamental front. Of all these, by far the most famous, is the one known from the Cuneiform inscription on it, to be that of Darius, the son of Hystaspes. It is situated at Nakhsh-i-Rustám, about four miles from Persepolis, and has near it another tomb of nearly the same character, though less richly ornamented. In their interiors these tombs show considerable differences. It is further worthy of note, that the tombs immediately above Persepolis, are more richly decorated than the others, the lintels and sideposts of the doors being covered with rosettes, and the entablature above the cornice bearing a row of lions facing one another, on each side toward the centre.

* Dan. viii. 2.

CHAPTER V.

Arsacidæ—Arsakes I—Tiridates I—Artabanus—Mithradates I—Phraates II—Scythian invasion--Mithradates II—Progress of the Romans—Orodes—Crassus—Pompey—Antony—Tiridates, son of Vologases—Trajanus—Avidius Cassius—Severus—Artabanus—Battle of Nisibis.

As already stated, with the death of Darius ends for more than five centuries the rule of native Persian sovereigns over more, perhaps, than the small province of Persis: I shall, therefore, now give some account of the Arsacidæ, whose vigorous rule fills up the intervening period.

It was in the reign of Antiochus Theos, the third of the Seleucidæ or Greek rulers of Syria and Mesopotamia, and about B.C. 250, that Askh or Arsaces slew the viceroy of Parthia, and spreading to the winds the sacred banner of the *Darafsh-i-Kawáni* (or Blacksmith's apron), which his uncle had saved, after the overthrow of Arbela, marched on Rhages (Rhey), at the same time inviting the other chieftains of his people to join with him in a revolt against the Greek kings of Syria.

Oriental writers claim Askh, though on no reliable grounds, as a descendant of the ancient kings of Persia; but it is more probable that his revolt was mainly due to the success of a similar uprising against the Seleucidæ a few years earlier, on the part of the Bactrian Diodotus, showing, as this did, the then weakened hold of the ruling family over their more distant provinces. The two revolts, however, differed essentially in their character; the one being of Greek against Greek, and under a Greek leader, the other "of an Asiatic race of a savage and rude type," against a more civilized and effeminate population. Besides this, there had been for years a tendency on the part of the Parthian tribes to separate themselves from the Persians, a tendency fostered, doubtless, in no small degree by the ancient enmity between the Magians and Zoroastrians. It was, in fact, the old story over again. As the Achæmenidæ, when they were strong, had tried to stamp out Magism, so the Magians retorted whenever they had the chance. The spring had, indeed, been pressed flat, yet had not lost its elasticity; and the fall of Darius Codomannus probably aroused new hopes for the down-trodden Magians, the more so that the Seleucid Greeks, "cared for none of these things." We must not, however, lay too much stress on the religious side of the question; no reformation such as that by the Achæmenian Darius or the Sassanian Ardashir, was dreamt of; indeed, the actual faith of the Parthians was lax and all-embracing, a mixture of Scythic dogmas, Greek practices, and Semitic ideas, while the hostility of the ruling families was rather anti-Persian than anything else. Thus we find the Parthians setting up the statues of Greek divinities and adopting Greek as the usual language of their coins, and affecting the titles of Phil-Hellenes, even when most hostile to the Greeks.

A revolt in many ways similar took place again, as we shall see, five hundred years afterwards, when, in its turn, the oppressive rule of the Arsacidæ had disgusted the subject population, and when, from wars and other causes, they held the reins of power with less vigor than at first : then it was, that the leaven of Zoroastrianism again swelled the masses, and the sceptre passed away from the house of Arsakes. It is likely, too, that the suppression or banishment of the Zoroastrian Magi,* or more purely native priesthood, had kept alive, especially in the more strictly Persian districts, during the whole period of the Arsacidan rule, an undying hatred of their oppressors; for the government of this family throughout was one of mere force ; the power of the chief monarch being supported by customs which exhibit some analogy with the feudal system of the Middle Ages.

About the year B.C. 150, we find the Arsacidan family divided into five principal branches. 1. That of Persia including Parthia, whose chief was always the admitted head of the rest, the "king of kings."

* The Magi, or priests of the religion of Zoroaster, must not be confounded with Magism, though, as we learn from the story of the Magophonia, Magus was the common name for the priests of Magism or elemental worship, as well as of Zoroastrianism. The Magi seem originally to have been a Median tribe (Herod. i. 101), but to have, subsequently, under the Persian rule, taken an active part in promoting Zoroastrianism.

2. That of Armenia. 3. That of Bactria and of the adjacent provinces. 4. That of Georgia. 5. That of the Massagetæ. Roughly speaking, it was a form of alliance, loosely enough interpreted, when there was no external foe, and liable to constantly recurring international feuds and wars. When, however, any of the separate provinces was threatened or assailed by an enemy from without, all alike joined to repel the common foe; hence, when Rome attacked Parthia, the outlying districts of Georgia and the Caucasus at once united in its defence. That such a system should have so long prevailed, implies no inconsiderable power of concentration, and it is likely it would have endured much longer than it did but for the exterminating wars with the Romans in which it was ultimately involved. Add to this, that many of the younger princes of the house had, by that time, tasted in Rome luxuries of which they had scant experience in their mountain homes, and (as Juvenal has remarked) had returned to Artaxata with habits very different from those of their frugal and hardy ancestors.*

The reign of Arsakes I., lasted only two years; and he can hardly be said to have secured his power

---

* I may here observe, *en passant*, that for the early history of the Arsacidæ, we are almost wholly indebted to the Roman writers, as we are for the later times to the Armenian chronicles: the Arsacidæ, indeed, left no personal memorial but their coins. The more modern Persian writers notice their rulers only as Muluk-al-Thuwaif, "Chiefs of bands." The Sháh-nameh of Firdúsi has only three or four pages for the whole 500 years of their history, while the Seleucidæ are not even mentioned,

when he was killed in battle. His successor, however, Tiridates I., was, fortunately for his family, a man of great ablility, and to him is due the consolidation of the empire of which Arsakes had laid the foundations.* With him, known in history as Arsakes II., arose the practice of double names for each monarch, the one his private, the other his dynastic designation; and as the Romano-Greek writers have preserved many of these private names, we are thus able to determine correctly most of their dates.

In the early part of his reign, Tiridates annexed Hyrcania, and, not long after, persuading the son of the Bactrian Diodotus to throw in his lot with him, the confederates completely defeated the whole forces of the Seleucid Callinicus. Can we wonder that the Parthians yearly celebrated, by a solemn anniversary, the remembrance of a victory, which must have been the result of a very unequal struggle? From this period till his death, Tiridates was peacefully employed in building his famous city of Dara or Dariæum, the site of which had not yet been discovered by the zeal or the imagination of Eastern travelers. His son and successor, Artabanus, taking advantage of a war between Antiochus III., and one

* The original centre of the Arsacidan rule, was around the middle of the Caspian Sea; and their advance into the valley of the Tigris was gradual. Moreover, though at times they held the whole country to the Persian Gulf, the foundation by Antiochus Theos of the town of Spasini-Kharax in B.C. 140, as it deprived them of a direct trade with India, so it prevented them from becoming a naval as well as military power.

of his satraps, Achæus, added to his dominions the district between Hyrcania and the Zagros mountains, the result being, as might have been anticipated, a war between the Parthians and the Seleucidæ, the details of which are wanting. In the end, however, we know that Antiochus of Syria made peace with his troublesome neighbor, and, by recognizing his independence, showed he had found his match, if not his superior, in the Parthian king. From this time to the close of the reign of Artabanus, we find nothing certain in Parthian history, nor is it worth while to attempt the unraveling of a skein so entangled.

With the reign of Mithradates I., (B.C. 174), Parthia takes a leap in advance, and acquires dimensions fully justifying Professor Rawlinson in the name he has given to it, of "The Sixth Oriental Monarchy." No doubt the conditions of the time favored the views of Mithradates, the Seleucidæ having then lost much of their original power, while their sceptre was in the hands of a boy, Eupator, with two rival claimants for the regency, Lysias and Philip. Mithradates, therefore, attacked Media, and after a vigorous resistance on the part of its inhabitants, secured for himself the great province of Media Magna. He next added to his dominions Hyrcania on the north, and Elymais or Susiana on the south; and, by the submission of the Persians and Babylonians, extended his monarchy from the Hindu-Kush to the Euphrates. How far Eastward he went is doubtful; but it has been thought that he did not stay his hand till he had annexed to his domains the Panjáb and head waters of the Indus.

On this point, however, so far as it is worth, numismatic evidence seems conclusive, as no Parthian coins have been found in this region; while, on the other hand, it is certain that Græco-Bactrian monarchs held Kábul and Western India, till at least B.C. 126. We may fairly believe that his sway extended over all the countries west of the Suleimán-Koh, a tract estimated by Professor Rawlinson as 1,500 miles, east and west, by a breadth in some parts more than 400 miles; no inconsiderable part of which comprises the most fertile regions of Middle and Western Asia. Envy, however, if no better reasons, suggested an attempt to reduce his power, and the Seleucid ruler Demetrius led an attack he perhaps thought would be acceptable to some of the aggrieved populations of the neighborhood. In this, however, he miscalculated alike their feelings and the real resources of the Parthian monarch. In one great battle his army was completely destroyed, and he himself was exhibited as a captive though, as it would seem, with the treatment due to his rank, through several of the provinces that had revolted; a warning to those who should in future attempt to thwart the new Asiatic empire.

After a thirty-eight years' glorious reign, which fully entitled him to adopt the proud designation of "King of kings," he was the first of the Parthians to assume, Mithradates died B. C. 136. This monarch was also the first to wear the tiara, or tall stiff crown, which, with some modifications, remained the royal head-dress till the final overthrow of the Sassanian dynasty by the Muhammedans, A. D. 641. Like the Achæmenian kings, those of the house of Arsakes occupied different residences according to the season of the year. Their winter they generally spent at Ctesiphon, and the rest of the year at Ecbatana (Hamadán), Tape in Hyrcania, or Rhages (Rhey).

Mithradates was succeeded by his son Phraates II., and a war with Syria would probably at once have broken out had not the then ruler of Syria, Antiochus Sidetes, been afraid to leave in his rear Judæa, which his predecessor Demetrius had openly declared independent. The independence, however, of the Jews did not last long, and, their ruler, John Hyrcanus, was compelled to admit the authority of the Syrian monarch, and to pay tribute, as before, in token of his submission (B. C. 133).* Antiochus then

* The gallant resistance of the Jews against Antiochus Epiphanes and the fearful end of that impious king are well told in 1 Maccab. iii. 4, and 2 Maccab. i. 9; yet, bad as he was, it seems to me that we are not bound to consider him, even as the Anti-Christ of the Old Testament. Certainly he opposed God, in that he was very zealous for his own false gods, as is abundantly shown by Polybius. The same fact is clear from the Bible—" King Antiochus wrote to his whole kingdom that all should be one people, and every one should leave his own laws" (1 Macc. i. 41, 42)—in others words, he wished to enforce an unbending state religion. But the true Anti-Christ would seem to be an apostate from the truth, not one, who, like a heathen, might exchange one error for another. His chief characteristics are self-exaltation, contempt of all religion, blasphemy against the true God, and apostacy from the God of his fathers.

proposed an attack on the Parthians, and at the first was completely successful, winning three battles in succession: in the end, however, the hardy mountaineers were too much for the enervated people of the plains, and Antiochus and his whole army were destroyed. Henceforward Parthia enjoyed, unmolested by the Seleucidæ the power it had acquired by honest fighting, indeed, the Greeks were scarcely able to maintain their now small domains of Cilicia and Syria Proper, encroached on as they were alike by Romans, Egyptians, and Arabs. In another sixty years, Syria became, as it might have been long before, a Roman province.

Phraates himself perished with the flower of his army in a conflict with the Scythians aided by a body of revolted Greeks. These Scythians, who had previously been in some measure allied to the Parthians (at least, so far as their wandering habits permitted),—were a portion of the great nomad hordes of Central Asia, who like the Cimmerii, to whom we have alluded, before historic times and often since, have swept down on the fertile, cultivated and comparatively refined south, like a whirlwind of locusts. Each country in its turn had to curse the presence of these savage and barbarous hosts, and Parthia had now to combat warriors as brave and as active as the best of her own people. To check their first advance the Parthian princes had paid them a sort of black mail; but Bactria, less fortunate, was rapidly overwhelmed to the north and west.

The Scythian tribes are known under several titles,

as the Massagetæ, Dahæ, Tochari and Sakarauli—and their manners and sometimes cannibal practices are fully recorded in Herodotus and Strabo. This time again the Scythians were superior in the conflict, and another Parthian king (Artabanus II.) was slain; but, on the accession of the next monarch, Mithradates II., termed, from his famous deeds, the Great, the tide of Scythian victory was arrested, and they were driven back, and compelled to pour their superabundant numbers into Seistan and the Eastern provinces of Persia.*

Thus was formed the famous Indo-Scythic kingdom, of whose chieftains we have so many monetary records. Occupying, as they did, the plains south of the Hindu-Kush between Bactria and the Panjáb, and occasionally extending their power even to the mouth of the Indus, this Scythian kingdom effectually separated India from Greece, and arrested the growing influence of Greek manners and civilization; indeed, but for these intervening hordes, there seems no reason why the Greek language should not have been as well understood on the Jumna and the Ganges as on the Nile. Having disposed of the Scyths, so far as his own country was concerned, Mithradates II. commenced his memorable wars with the Armenians, a people originally of the same Turanian origin with the Parthians themselves, but, in

* The present name of this portion of Persia, Seistán (or on the coins Sejestán) is a memorial of this Scythic invasion, the district they occupied having been naturally called Sacastene—the land of the Sacæ.

later years, owing to a considerable infusion of Aryan elements, the faithful allies, as a rule, of the Achæmenidæ. The first independence of Armenia dates from B. C. 190, the year in which Antiochus the Great was defeated by the Romans; but, a few years afterwards, Armenia became again for a short time subject to the Seleucidæ. No details of the war between Mithradates II. and the Armenians have been preserved, but there can be but little doubt that their resistance to the Parthians was as brief as it was unsuccessful.

Another event was, however, now about to take place, which changed the whole character of Eastern affairs, and brought into the plains of Asia a race of warriors unsurpassed by even the Macedonians of Alexander. The course of their previous war in Greece had enabled the Roman leaders to read distinctly their future destiny, though they did not at first follow out the line so clearly traced for them. When the consul, Acilius Glabrio, was about to drive the forces of Antiochus from that pass which, as has been remarked, "was never stormed, and whose only conqueror has been nature," he addressed his soldiers in an oration plainly demonstrating the views of these ambitious republicans. "What," said he, "shall hinder, but that from Gades to the Red Sea we should have but one boundary, the ocean, who holds the whole circuit of the earth in his embraces; and that the whole race of men should venerate the Roman name, as second only to the gods?" Now it was, that Latin, "the voice of empire and of war, the true language of history, instinct with the spirit of nations, and not with the passions of individuals," bade fair to become what its half-sister, the Greek, was already, the common tongue of the civilized world.

To the unbending rule of Rome, each nation in its turn was to yield; republics in Europe, monarchies in Asia, the cavalry of the East, the foot soldiers of the West—all alike were now to be frozen up in one iron uniformity. "The mistress of the world," says Wilberforce, "sent forth her prætors and proconsuls to rule instead of kings; vast roads, uniform and unbending, were the tracks she made for herself through the world, that so the most inaccessible countries might be laid open to her armies; and, in making them, she hewed through mountains and filled up vallies, as though the earth was as subject to her as its inhabitants."

Hitherto, the interposition of the kingdom of Syria, and of the provinces of Cappadocia and Armenia, had prevented actual contact between the Romans and the Parthians; but their mutual progress was continually bringing them nearer; while another great power, too, had about the same time sprung up in the same neighborhood, that of Mithradates V., of Pontus, the son of a former ally of Rome, whose rise was perhaps more sudden and more remarkable than that of any other of the kings of Western Asia. Hostile as he was, alike to Roman and Parthian, it was but natural that a joint effort should be made by the latter power and Rome, to repress the new and common enemy; hence an embassy from the Parthian Mithradates II., to Sylla, shortly after the defeat of the Cappadocians by the Romans, an embassy perhaps stimulated by the fact that Tigranes of Armenia had attached himself to the cause of the king of Pontus, and had taken from Parthia the whole of Upper Mesopotamia. Sylla, however, did not at once fall in with this scheme, and the Parthian Mithradates II., soon after died, after a reign of more than thirty-five years.

For some years after this event, it is not clear who was the actual ruler of Parthia; but during this period the great war between the Romans and Mithradates of Pontus was in progress, the obvious policy of the Parthians being to keep aloof, and to amuse both sides with fair words and empty promises; in the end, however, Phraates III., made an alliance with Pompey, and marching into Armenia while the Roman general was occupied with Mithradates, was completely successful. But Pompey, perhaps not choosing at the time to give additional strength to any Asiatic prince, not only failed to reward Phraates for his services, but drove the Parthians out of Gordyene (or Upper Mesopotamia), which had always been considered an integral part of their empire, while he at the same time refused to the Parthian monarch his now customary title of "King of kings." As each party, apparently, had a wholesome dread of the other, war, though often imminent, did not break out, and a proposal for arbitration on the part of Pompey was accepted. Phraates soon after this was assassinated, about B.C. 61, and another period of confusion in Parthian history arose.

Orodes, the next monarch of note, ascended the throne about B.C. 56, just as Crassus announced his intention of carrying the Roman arms across the Euphrates. But the Parthian monarch was not to be caught sleeping, and made good use of nearly two years in completing his preparation against the invader. Indeed, Crassus, even after he had reached Syria, seemed in no hurry to commence the attack; hence the first campaign passed away uselessly, while in the second he would, perhaps, have hardly taken the initiative, had he not been provoked by the taunts of a Parthian ambassador to march like a madman across Mesopotamia, through an arid, trackless district, where he was exposed to incessant assaults by the innumerable cavalry of his enemy. He was also opposed by the ablest Parthian general of the time, Surena,* who, at the age of less than thirty years, had been entrusted by the Parthian king with his best troops.

The Parthian, like the Persian cavalry, was of two classes, one, a body lightly armed with only a bow of great strength, and a quiver of arrows; the other, a body of heavy cavalry, with horses, like

---

* It was long thought that Ammianus was right in supposing Surena, or Surenas, a title rather than a proper name, in fact, that of the personage next in rank to the king himself (xxiv. 2), while Appian supposed this title hereditary in the family of the Surena who conquered Crassus. The Armenian records show that it was really the name of one of the leading families among the Parthians.

their riders, clad in armor, and carrying a long and heavy spear, more powerful and weightier than even the *pilum* of the Romans. The armament of Surena was almost wholly cavalry, but probably of both classes; he had besides, an invaluable aid in a traitor named Abgarus, who, himself commanding a body of light horse in the service of Crassus, revealed to his countrymen the Roman plans, as fast as they were formed. At length the two armies met, and the Romans had their first experience of the special tactics of their new enemies, who, completely enveloping them with their cavalry, plied them with a ceaseless discharge of arrows. In vain they attempted to advance : as they rushed forward, the Parthians fell back just as suited best their mode of fighting, destroying utterly by a stratagem, some 6000 Gaulish troops under the son of Crassus. On the next day but one, the remnant of the Roman army capitulated, on the death of their general, Crassus, in a chance melée, occasioned by an attempt on the part of the Parthians, to capture him during a conference with Surena. "Of the entire army," says Professor Rawlinson, "which had crossed the Euphrates, consisting of about 40,000 men, not more than a fourth returned. One half of the whole number perished."

It is said, that the news and the bloody head of Crassus reached Orodes, while watching, with Artavasdes, the acting of the "Bacchæ" of Euripides, his intended war with the Armenian chief having been changed into matrimonial festivities. Florus and Dio add the more questionable story, that the Parthians, believing the expedition of Crassus to have sprung from mere lust of plunder, poured melted gold into his mouth. It may be remarked, in conclusion, that the result of this great victory was by no means what might have been anticipated, as Orodes did not follow it up, but wasted much valuable time in the siege of various towns (an operation of rare success, when performed by Asiatic troops).

We hear little more of Orodes, till when, a few years later, Pompey was, on his part, desirous of an alliance which might strengthen him against his great adversary, Cæsar: but the terms Orodes demanded, the absolute surrender of the whole province of Syria, were obviously such as no Roman could accept; and, though, after Pharsalia, Cæsar professed his intention of carrying the war into Parthia, that country was spared by the daggers of the conspirators from open conflict with the greatest general of his age.

Nor was this all: the quarrels among the Triumvirs gave the Parthians the hope of securing some portion of the Roman dominions in the East, especially as Antony, after having alienated many of the Eastern nations by his exactions, had retired to Egypt. They, too, had at that time with them a Roman general of some reputation, the younger Labienus, who, like his father, having supported the cause of Pompey, had a reasonable dread of the proscriptions of the victors. Hence a characteristic outburst, in which their hosts of cavalry overran a great portion of Syria, taking even such towns as Apamæa and Antioch, and a further raid by the Parthian king (Pacorus) himself, into Phœnicia and Palestine, and by Labienus into Asia Minor. In this war Jerusalem submitted to the indignity of receiving as its ruler Antigonus, the last of the Asmonæan princes, from the hands of Pacorus, who had been bribed to espouse his cause against John Hyrcanus by the gifts of 1000 talents and 500 Jewish women: the spectacle was then witnessed of its last priest-king, sitting on the throne of David, from B.C. 40 to B.C. 37, as the satrap and dependent vassal of a foreign monarchy.

But these successes were of short duration. In the autumn of B.C. 39, the lieutenant of Antony, Ventidius, in a campaign of remarkable rapidity and brilliancy, cleared Syria of the invaders, and, in the following spring, completely routed the Parthian army and slew Pacorus. Indeed, it is manifest throughout their whole history, that, for long-sustained efforts the Parthians were no match for the Romans; their military system, never varying, lacked elasticity and the power of adaptation to new and changing circumstances; and, though admirably adapted for the great plains of Asia, failed in more contracted and difficult regions. Hence, when Rome, to meet her new enemy, changed her armament accordingly, the Parthians gave up their previous policy of aggression, preferring rather to stand at bay than to commence the attack: it was a wiser if not a nobler plan, to defend their territories from invasion, and to this Parthia consistently adhered during the remaining two centuries and a half of her existence as a separate monarchy.

When, a little later, Orodes, like so many of his predecessors, perished by assassination, Antony, hearing that his son and successor, Phraates, with his hands imbrued in the blood of father and subjects, alike, had alienated from him many of his chief nobles, thought the opportunity had come for avenging the losses of the Roman arms under Crassus, and of exalting his own fame and renown. But he was destined to meet with a chastisement, less fatal, indeed, than that of Crassus, yet scarcely less humiliating. Advancing rashly by forced marches to Phraaspa, and still more rashly dividing his forces at that place, he allowed the Parthians to close upon his lieutenant, Oppius Stasianus, to destroy his army and more than ten thousand Romans, and to capture his baggage and munitions of war. Nor was this all: Artavasdes, the monarch of Armenia who had been mainly instrumental in inducing Antony to attempt this perilous march, with true Oriental instinct deserted his Roman friend, in the belief that the Roman cause was now desperate.

The position indeed of Antony was one of the utmost danger: and he had no alternative but to fall back on the Araxes, harassed, for nineteen consecutive days, in every way the Parthians could harass him, without allowing themselves to be drawn into a pitched battle. At length, after a march of

277 English miles, the Romans crossed the "unbridged" Araxes, at the ferry of Julfa,* and found themselves in the comparatively friendly land of Armenia, though with the loss of not less than 30,000 men. In the following year, B.C. 35, Antony, who had spent the winter at Alexandria, repaid the treachery of the Armenian Artavasdes by over-running his country, and capturing him with an incredible amount of booty; a natural, but unwise, act of retaliation, as it at once drove the Armenians to make common cause with the Parthians, and thus united two powerful provinces which a shrewder policy would have kept apart.

Some years later (B.C. 20) Augustus† received back the standards taken from Crassus, the then Parthian

* Virgil's "pontem indignatus Araxes" (Æn. viii. 728), refers to a few years later, when Tiberius, as lieutenant of Augustus, certainly penetrated into the heart of Armenia. It may, however, be doubted whether, even then, the Romans built a bridge over the Araxes, but they were the only engineers then who could have done so. Certainly they did not do it under the feeble rule of Honorius, as Claudian would have us believe.

† It was in B.C. 22 that Augustus first publicly announced his expedition to the East, but personally did no more than encamp his army along the Euphrates. Tiberius had, however, by this time marched into Armenia, for Horace speaks of the submission of the "Cold Niphates" (doubtless *Nebad*, or Ararat) and of the "river of the Medes" (Od. i. 2)—and it may be, that a successful battle near Ararat, in the heart of Armenia, hastened the return of the captured standards. Horace probably uses a poet's license when he makes Phraates on his knees re-accept his kingdom from Augustus (Epist. i. 12); but it is nevertheless certain that Augustus carried the four sons of Phraates to Rome, leaving a fifth, and illegitimate one, to poison the Parthian king.

king, Phraates, being well aware that he could not resist such a force as the Roman Emperor could have brought against him. Many years of comparative peace then ensued, as the immediate successors of Augustus adhered faithfully to his judgment, that the Roman empire had reached its limits: nor, indeed, was it till Trajan again awakened the dream of universal empire, that any serious struggle took place between Rome and Parthia. It is not necessary to notice here several petty wars about this period, most of which may be traced to the weakness and vacillation of the Armenian princes or of their subjects. I ought, however, to mention that, during this interval, a new race had become involved in the various conflicts of the times, with a capacity as soldiers the Romans were long unwilling to admit. Vast numbers of Jews were now spread over Western Asia. Some, probably the descendants of the colonies planted by the kings of Assyria and Babylon, others dwellers from choice in the countries adjacent to Palestine, as the Parthians, were generally tolerant, especially when toleration promoted their commercial interests. "They formed," says Professor Rawlinson, "a recognized community, had some cities which were entirely their own, possessed a common treasury, and, from time to time, sent up to Jerusalem the offerings of the people under the protection of a convoy of 30,000 or 40,000 men." In fact the Parthians must have felt that this Jewish population was, in some degree, a counterpoise to the disaffected Greeks, Armenians, and Syrians.

The only other event of importance at this period was the quarrel between Vologases and the Romans which led to several attacks by the Parthians on Armenia, but is chiefly remarkable for the visit of his son Tiridates to Rome, an event as curious as it is strange. It appears that after the recovery of Armenia by the Romans, Corbulo, the Roman general, insisted that Tiridates should proceed to Rome and receive his crown direct from the hands of Nero, while he detained one of his sisters as a hostage that this act should be fully carried into execution. We learn that after a while Tiridates set out, accompanied by his wife and an escort of 3000 Parthian cavalry, that passing through two-thirds of the empire they were everywhere received as though in a triumphal procession, and that great cities turned out to welcome them and hung their streets with festive garlands. After riding on horseback the whole way, through Thrace and Illyricum, on their reaching Rome, the whole city was illuminated on the night before the investiture, and, on the following day, the Armenian prince ascended the rostra, and seated himself at the feet of the emperor. As Professor Rawlinson has well put it, "The circumstance of his journey and reception involved a concession to Rome of all that could be desired in the way of formal or verbal acknowledgment. The substantial advantage, however, remained with the Parthians. The Romans, both in the East and at the capital, were flattered by a show of submission; but the Orientals must have concluded that the long struggle had terminated in an acknowledgment by Rome of Parthia as the stronger power." The establishment of the Parthian Tiridates as king of Armenia, secured a considerable period of peace between Rome and Armenia; hence there is little to record here, except another irruption from the north by a Scythian named Alaric in A.D. 78, which gave the opportunity of revolt to the Hyrcanians and was thus the first step towards the disruption of the long sway of the Arsacidæ.

For the first years of his reign Trajan was sufficiently occupied by the nations of the West; but, in A.D. 114, having conquered Dacia, he resolved to reassert the dominion of Rome in Asia, much weakened as this had been during the reigns of his unwarlike predecessors. The times too had greatly changed since the conquests of Lucullus and Antony, and new elements of confusion had arisen, tending to disintegrate still further the already partially collapsing rule of the Parthians. Christianity was already acting "as a dissolvent on the previously existing forms of society," and Judaism, "embittered by persecution, had from a nationality become a conspiracy."

To avert the meditated attack of Trajan, the ambassador of the ruler of Armenia, Chosroes, met him at Athens, and tried by rich gifts to come to any arrangement short of invasion ; but Trajan had resolved on a campaign, in which he hoped to emulate, if not surpass, the deeds of Alexander. His chance, however, of any such distinction was small, as the forces of the Eastern princes were no longer what they had been, when they crushed Crassus and humbled Antony. No Orodes or Phraates III. held the sceptre of the East; hence, when Trajan had passed Samosata, he was not stayed on his onward course, though Parthamasiris, the Parthian ruler, in the most abject manner, divesting his brow of his diadem, laid it at the feet of the emperor. It was evidently the opinion of Trajan that such submission was simply a matter of course, deserving little praise or thanks, still less reward; the Parthian was simply to do the bidding of Rome. Nor, indeed, had this been all, would there have been much to remark about it; it would have been but another instance of the weaker going to the wall. But, as all will regret, Trajan was not content with the submission of the young prince, but shortly afterwards put him to death. As the whole character of Trajan is averse to petty assassinations, it is but fair to suppose that, in this instance, he was misled by false or doubtful rumors, the more so as he had the courage to avow that this deed was wholly his own, and therefore probably believed it a necessary act of justice.

The general result of the first campaign was, that Greater and Lesser Armenia were formed into one province, and the nations taught that Rome was the power they had most to dread. In the same year Mesopotamia was in like manner reduced, while in that following (A.D. 116) the provincial towns of Nineveh,* Gaugamela, and Arbela, fell into the

* It is supposed that the Roman colony of Nineveh was founded

K

hands of the Romans, the whole tract between the Zagros and the Tigris having been over-run ; other places, too, of great importance, as Hatra and Ctesiphon, submitted, and there seemed no limit to Roman conquest.

But the Parthian well knew his advantages ; if he could not fight in the open field, he could fall back as the Roman advanced, and leave a desert behind him, impracticable for even Roman military genius. Above all, while Trajan, the first and the last emperor to do so, was lamenting, on the waters of the Indian Ocean, that his advanced age alone prevented his adding India to his conquests, the Parthian could foment disaffection in his rear, and thus compel the vain-glorious conqueror to retrace his steps through the half-subdued regions behind him. Hence, too, willing instruments of the Parthian policy, the populace of Seleucia, Hatra, and Nisibis, rose in arms behind him, and it is likely that his retreat would have been cut off had his lieutenants been less equal to their duties, or unable to crush at its commencement the spreading rebellion. In spite of this, however, Trajan was compelled to beat a hasty retreat and to acknowledge that his power over these Eastern provinces was little better than a rope of sand: nay, what must have grieved him more than anything else, he had to submit to a humiliating repulse

by Claudius. Coins of this place exist with the name of Niniva Claudiopolis, under the emperors Trajan, Maximinus, Severus, Alexander, Mamæa, and Gordianus Pius (Num. 1 Chron. xix..1). Tacitus and Ammianus also notice it.

by the rude Arabs of Hatra, his troops being unable or unwilling to force their way, though their engines had breached its walls. In the next year, A.D. 117, Trajan died, and his successor, Hadrian, deeming his conquests impolitic, at once forbore extending the Eastern frontiers of the empire. Hadrian, in fact, voluntarily relinquished the three provinces Trajan's Parthian war had added to the empire. "Rome, therefore," as Professor Rawlinson remarks, "gained nothing by the great exertions she had made, unless it were a partial recovery of her lost influence in Armenia."

The next direct conflict between the Romans and the Parthians in the reign of Vologases III., is so far worthy of record that it is the first occasion in which a Roman army had been completely successful in its invasion: it is also noteworthy that the general who accomplished this feat seems to have acted on his own authority, and without any direct orders from Rome. The circumstances were these: a petty war had arisen, owing to the raid of the Alani into the province of Cappadocia, which had been, however, crushed for the time by the historian, Arrian, then its Prefect. But a little later, about the year A.D. 161, the war became more general, Parthian troops having crossed the Euphrates, and pushed on through Syria, into Palestine. To meet these invaders, the young, pleasure-loving and incompetent Verus was sent from Rome to take the chief command, but associated with him were able officers, the ablest being Avidius Cassius. This officer had at first a difficult task before him, but, at length, in A.D. 163, he routed the Parthian king in a great battle at Europus, and drove him across the Euphrates. Nor was he slow to follow up his first success. Having won another considerable battle near Susa, he besieged, took, and burnt Seleucia on the right bank of the Tigris, and occupied Ctesiphon on the left. Thence, still advancing, he crossed the Zagros, and, seizing part of Media, enabled his imperial masters to add to their already assumed titles of "Armeniacus" and "Parthicus," the new one of "Medicus."

Parthia was thus for the time completely humbled; yet had cause for abundant rejoicing in the fate that ultimately befell her invaders. In Babylonia a disease, alike unwonted and wasting, was contracted by the soldiers; a scourge, indeed, so terrible that their deaths were numbered by thousands; and, what was worse, the survivors, on their homeward march, carried the infection with them, till the pestilence had swept over Italy and reached even the shores of the Atlantic Ocean. If Eutropius can be believed, nearly one-half of the whole population and almost all the Roman army were carried off by it. Yet by this war, fatal as it had been to the conquerors, a province of Parthia, that between the Euphrates and the Khabur, became Roman, and was long held by the emperors as part of the Roman territory. The struggle ended in A.D. 165, and, though Vologases survived another twenty-five years, he did not make any effective effort to recover the ground he had lost. Indeed, the Parthian system was now on its decline, and the time was fast maturing for the substitution in its place of a revived religion. The next time we find the Parthians at war with Rome was, when, on the death of Commodus, the empire was claimed by Pescennius Niger, Clodius Albinus, and Severus, respectively. During these disturbances, the Parthians naturally gave their aid where it was likely to be most damaging to the Roman empire; probably caring little enough which individual became emperor, so only he entered on his government with diminished forces and strength.

In the progress of these commotions, Sept. Severus marched twice across Mesopotamia; in his second expedition, perhaps hoping to surpass Trajan, he built a fleet in the upper country, and captured the great cities of Babylon, Seleucia, and Ctesiphon. But here his successes ended. In spite of his usual care, supplies began to be scarce, and Severus felt the necessity of falling back ere a greater calamity should befall him. As the country along the Euphrates had been entirely exhausted, Severus retired along the banks of the Tigris; on his way, however, meeting with a repulse at Hatra, not unlike that which had befallen Trajan, and which completely tarnished all his previous victories. Hatra was, at that time, reputed to be full of treasure, so the covetous emperor resolved to plunder it, in return, as he pretended, for the aid the people had given to his rival Niger. The place, though small, was surrounded by a solid wall, on which the Roman engines made little impression; the people were brave and skilful archers; moreover had a body of cavalry who cut to pieces the Roman foraging parties. The result was that they withstood two sieges, the last of twenty days; till, at length, Severus was compelled to retire, with his army demoralized and suffering from diseases, the natural effect of a march during the hottest season of the year, with an inadequate supply of wholesome food. His troops, indeed, we are told, openly refused to obey his orders, and shrunk from the actual assault, though the breach was deemed practicable.

But, though Severus failed to reduce Hatra, there can be no doubt that, on the whole, his expedition was glorious for Rome, as by it another province was taken from the Parthians; in fact he not only recovered Rome's former position in Mesopotamia, but, by crossing the Tigris, secured also the fertile tract of Adiabene between the northern Záb and the Adhem. By this advance he established the Roman power within less than seventy miles of the Parthian capital, and provided means for an easy descent, when necessary, upon the still greater cities of Babylon and Seleucia. During the whole of this prolonged conflict in Mesopotamia we do not hear of any Parthian resistance, and must therefore suppose either that Vologases IV., had not the power to interfere, or that his people no longer possessed the enthusiastic bravery of their more youthful empire.

On his death, about A.D. 209, and for the next seventeen or eighteen years preceding the revolt of the Persians, it is clear from the coins that his two sons, Artabanus and Vologases were reigning, though it is impossible to say with certainty over what parts of the country. As the Roman writers, after the year A.D. 215, speak of Artabanus only, and give this name to the last Parthian king, it may be presumed that in him was vested the chief power, and that he, at all events, was the personage whom the Western nations recognized as the chief ruler. There is little of interest to notice in these years, except a strange and almost ludicrous proposal on the part of Caracalla, to wed a Parthian princess, with the view of dividing the conquest of the whole world between Rome and Parthia. "The Roman infantry," said he, "is the best in the world, and, in steady, hand-to-hand fighting, must be allowed to be unrivalled. The Parthians surpass all nations in the number of their cavalry and in the excellence of their archers."

There seems some doubt as to the reply Artabanus made, and Dio and Herodian differ on this point. It is, however, certain that Caracalla went as a friend with his army to Ctesiphon, and then, with characteristic treachery, fell on the unsuspecting Parthians, plundered and ravaged their territory, and returned to Mesopotamia laden with his ill-gotten spoil. The "common enemy of mankind," as Gibbon justly calls him, then disgraced the Roman name still further, by a wanton act of barbarity and insult, the destruction of the graves of the Parthian royal family, for ages preserved at Arbela. Not long after Caracalla was murdered, and his successor,

Macrinus, found himself at once opposed to a vast host, collected by Artabanus to avenge the insults his country had received from Caracalla. A prolonged battle of three days ensued near Nisibis, in which, having been completely worsted, Macrinus was compelled to restore the captives and booty carried off by Caracalla, and to purchase for something like a million and a half of our money, an ignominious peace with his great Asiatic rival. Thus ended the last conflict between Rome and Parthia; and, within a brief period, ended also the illustrious dynasty of the Arsacidæ by the death of Artabanus, A.D. 226, on the revolt of the Persians under Artaxerxes or Ardashír, of the house of Sassan, whence they derived their historical title of Sassanidæ. Professor Rawlinson well remarks of the Arsacidæ, "The race itself does not seem to have become exhausted. Its chiefs, the successive occupants of the throne, never sank into mere weaklings or fainéants; never shut themselves up in their seraglios or ceased to take a leading part alike in civil broils and in struggles with foreign rivals." It is, however, probable that their troops had ceased to be what they had been under the great early monarchs of the house, while there can be no question that their original empire, as created by Mithradates and others, had been much reduced.

Hyrcania, as we have seen, had revolted so early as A.D. 78, and, as far as we know, had maintained its own from that time, while the Romans had secured two at least of the most valuable of the western provinces of Parthia. Nor, indeed, did Rome altogether lose her prestige by the loss of the great battle of Nisibis, for, immediately after this action, Artabanus, in his treaty with Macrinus, surrendered the old Parthian province of Mesopotamia.

CHAPTER VI.

Sassanidæ — Ardashír I. — Shahpúr I. — Valerian — Odænathus— Varahrán II.—Tiridates of Armenia—Galerius—Narses—Shahpúr II.—Julian III.—Firúz I.—Nushírwán—Mauricius—Khosrú II. — Heraclius—Muhammed—Yezdigird III.—Muhammedan Conquest — Sassanian Monuments at Nakhsh-i-Rustám — Nakhsh-i-Regib—Shahpúr—Takht-i-Bostán—Mr. Thomas's interpretation of the inscriptions at Hajiábád.

IT is not easy to determine from such documents as have come down to us, all the motives that led to the Sassanian revolt, but the attentive student will observe abundant inducements for any man of real ability to take up arms against the then existing authorities and system. Indeed, there can be little doubt that there had long rankled in the hearts of the Persian people a hatred of their Arsacidan governors, though there was nothing especially oppressive in their rule, while they were, perhaps from indifference, generally tolerant in religious matters: moreover, in the earlier times, perhaps always, they had permitted the existence of native rulers over the province of Persis, which implies the recognition to some extent of the native manners and customs.

Yet at all periods the Persians must have resented their exclusion from the higher offices of the state, which the Arsacidæ jealously maintained for their own families and immediate followers; while they may also have felt that a nation, who had given to the world a Cyrus and a Darius, deserved some special pre-eminence. The Parthians could have had no inherent claim to the exclusive rule of Western Asia, and must, therefore, always have maintained their position by the mere force of arms: on the other hand, the Magi, as representing the faith of Zoroaster, would have had but little influence in Parthia, even if they had not been repressed by the strong arm of the civil power.

Again, the effect of the battle of Nisibis, though one of victory to the Arsacidæ, must really have been a source of weakness to them, or Artabanus would have at once followed it up by the destruction of Macrinus' army rather than by the cession of Mesopotamia to the Romans. It is further note-worthy that Moses of Chorene remarks that, at the same time, two princes of the house of Arsaces, who dwelt in Bactria, were at feud with the reigning monarch.

It has been supposed by some that the Ardashír who raised the standard of revolt was himself a Magus, and therefore directly bound to exert himself to the utmost in the defence of his own faith. On the other hand, Herodian asserts that he was at the time the tributary ruler of Persis. The early writers as Gibbon, and Malcolm, have taken the former view, Professor Rawlinson the latter. Perhaps all that is really certain on this subject is, that he was the son of a certain Sassan, and that his revolt against the Arsacidæ in Persis dates from about A.D. 220.

Before, however, I proceed to give some account of the principal Sassanian rulers, it is necessary to make a few remarks on their connection and dealings with the different populations with whom, during the 400 years of their dominion, they came in contact: bearing always in mind the fact, that the Persians claimed to be pure Iranians of the great Indo-European stock, though, doubtless, a good deal mixed with the non-Aryans (or Turanians), who dwelt around them. Unluckily, we have but few materials for the early part of their history. Native or contemporary chronicles there are none; and the later writers of Armenia or Constantinople are the records of enemies; the Armenians in those days always so, the Greeks generally. Yet to the latter we must trust entirely for the first hundred years and more, though, with this advantage, that some of them, like Ammianus and Procopius, took part in the scenes they describe; moreover, both of these, as well as Theophylact Simocatta, are on the whole, trustworthy.

On the other hand, though Armenian literature in any form did not commence till the fourth century A.D., as the old Armenians (the present people are Iranians who have forgotten their parentage) lived, from Achæmenian times, nearer to Persia than any other nation, it is reasonable to expect that from even their comparatively late writings, some names hitherto misconceived may be explained. Thus, I have already pointed out how the Greek writers generally assume that Surena or Surenas, was the title of the chief general under the monarch himself, if not his own second title; while the Armenian writers declare it was really the name of one of the great Arsacidan families who preserved their traditional lineage long after the empire had passed from their house. We meet with other and similar great families, as the Aspahapats (the Ispéhébids of the seventh and eighth centuries), and the Mihráns.

Other points worthy of notice, as explanatory of many confused passages in the history of the wars between the Greeks and the Persians, are the certain, clear, and definite objects every Sassanian ruler kept constantly before his eyes. These were, speaking generally, to extend the boundaries of the Persian empire to the west of the Euphrates; to weaken, whenever opportunity occurred, Armenia, as the northern frontier and the key of Persia, held as this state was at that period, by a population at variance from the Persians in creed and race; to prevent the progress of Christianity, not alone in their own dominions, but in the provinces adjacent to them; and to spread, by all possible means, the pure faith of Zoroaster, as distinguished from nature worship on one side and Christianity on the other. These principles borne in mind explain much of the subsequent history of this people. Thus, when Armenia was in league with the Byzantine Court, the Persians generally turned their arms against her, and less rarely into the provinces of the west and south: on the other hand, when Armenia and Persia were allied and friendly, or the former subject to the latter, the war was centralized in Mesopotamia or extended into Asia Minor, the northern frontiers of Persia being then secure. In every instance we find the Persians endeavoring to make sure of Armenia, and unwilling to join in wars distant from their own centre till they had complete control over the frontier mountains.

Again in their dealings with Christianity the Persian rulers were characteristically perfidious; and if fair and open enmity did not succeed, rarely scrupled to adopt any other means to sap its foundations. As is well known, the Greek Church from the fourth to the end of the sixth century, was rent by every form of controversy and religious fanaticism, followed as these are invariably by the bitter religious animosities; the emperors themselves had their share, too, in many of these quarrels, while œcumenical councils failed to reduce the factions to unity, often, perhaps, because the distances were so great and intercommunication so difficult. All these were sources of division among the Christians, and sources, too, of weakness; and the Persian rulers fostered both and profited by both; their object being to give their utmost support to any sect in arms against the orthodoxy of Constantinople. Thus, when the Nestorians were ejected from the schools of Edessa, they found a hearty welcome among the Sassanians of Persia; Firúz, the then monarch, seizing, in their behalf, the episcopal chair of Ctesiphon, the seat of the Patriarch of Assyria and Persia; while many other bishoprics shortly after fell into his hands, till nearly all Persia was Nestorianized.

In fact, the ordinary system of Persia gave full toleration to any creeds at variance with that of Constantinople, and, perhaps, in this aspect only, had any bond of union with the Armenians. Yet it must be admitted that Persian notions of toleration were meagre in kind and seldom long enduring. It was rare for even Nestorian Christianity to escape without persecution, except for some temporary political reason. Even the king of Persia, Kobád, lost his throne for embracing the views of Mazdak, and Mani (the author of Manicheism) was executed in Persia for inventing a mixed system of Zoroastrianism and Christianity. Again, in the same spirit, in which they used their utmost power to prevent the increase of converts to true and orthodox Christianity, the early Persian monarchs labored hard to collect together the scattered fragments of the Zend-avesta and of other works believed to embody Zoroastrian doctrines, and to set up on high abundant fire altars, the living memorials of their ancient faith. To the same end, they re-introduced Pehlevi as the Court language, re-constituted the body-guards called the "immortals," and, having somewhere found the old Darafsh-i-kawáni, again set it up as the banner of their renewed empire. Even the royal names of many of their most distinguished monarchs were taken directly from heroes recorded in the Zend-avesta, such as Ardashír, Khosúr, Kobád, Varahrán, and Ormazd.

We have stated that Ardashír probably took up arms about A.D. 220, and naturally, his first effort was to establish his authority in Persis,* and thence to conquer the adjacent and thinly-peopled district of Caramania or Kirmán, and ultimately Media. This last onslaught was perhaps induced by the belief that the Medians and Bactrians had given shelter to the two princes of the house of Arsaces to whom we have already alluded.

It would seem that, for some time, Artabanus made no attempt to put down the rebels; he now, however, marched an army into Persis, but was defeated in three great battles, and in the last, according to Malcolm, fought in the plain of Hormuz, between Bekahán and Shuster, he lost his life and crown, A.D. 226. By degrees all the provinces of the old Parthian empire fell into the hands of Ardashír, who, to give the color of legitimacy to his new empire, is said to have married an Arsacide princess,†

---

* I have noticed before, that owing to the position of Mesene (for many years under its own kings), the Parthians were never able for long to keep a navy afloat on the waters of the Persian Gulf. Owing to this circumstance a considerable commerce had sprung up with India on the one side and Petra on the other, during the first two centuries of our era. To secure, therefore this province was a necessity for Ardashír I., and one of his first operations was to build in Mesene, according to Hamzah of Ispahan (who wrote in the tenth century), a number of towns for commercial or naval purposes. One of these (rather rebuilt than built) was Forath-Maisan, a name, probably, recalling that of the old province, Mesene. It was the obvious policy of the petty kings of Mesene to be as neutral as possible in the wars between Rome and Parthia, seeing that they had in their hands so large a portion of the commerce of the Persian Gulf.

† It is right to add that coins exist of a certain Artavasdes, bearing the date of A.D. 227, but we have no clear evidence where he

The reign of Ardashír (sometimes called Babekán) was brilliant and successful. He was able to unite and to consolidate the various fragments of his empire; to contend with varying success against the Romans under Severus Alexander and to establish in its purity Zoroastrianism in opposition to the nature worship of the Arsacides.* The coins of the Sassanian dynasty, which abound, completely confirm the testimony of history. On all of them, we find the symbols of fire worship, the altar and his attendant priests, their legends being no longer in Greek, as those of the Arsacidæ, but in the ancient language of Persia.

Ardashír was succeeded by his son, Shahpúr I. (A.D. 240), who worthily carried out his father's schemes. After a brief war with an Arabian chief who had, during his absence in Khorassán, seized Jezireh (Mesopotamia), and fortified himself in the fortress of Al Hathr (Hatra), which had, as we have seen, already successfully defied the arms of Trajan and Severus, he passed on to Nisibis, carrying terror and devastation into the Roman provinces on the

reigned. In the northern districts, it appears from the Armenian chronicles, that the struggle was prolonged for some time, Khosrú, the then king of Armenia, having raised an army of Georgians and Huns, with whom he devastated Assyria as far south as Ctesiphon. Khosrú is said to have been victorious for ten years. On his murder, in A.D. 252, the Arsacidan rule in Armenia finally ended.

* Gibbon has further stated (though he does not quote his authority) that Ardashír was recognized in a solemn assembly at Balkh. If so, he must have subdued Bactria, but strictly speaking, this province was not absorbed into Persia till the reign of Julian, 130 years later.

L

Euphrates and Tigris. The siege of Nisibis was long and tedious, but, at length, according to Persian writers, Heaven heard the prayers of their devout emperor, and the walls of the city, like those of Jericho, yielded to religious influence what they had refused to military genius. Pursuing his conquests, Carrhæ fell before his victorious arms, and, shortly afterwards, in a great battle between him and the aged Valerian, the Roman emperor was himself taken prisoner near Edessa, A.D. 260, together with a large part of his army.* It is not certain what became of Valerian, and the stories of his cruel treatment by Shahpúr are probably exaggerated; but on the sculptures at the ruins of Shahpúr near Kazerún, and at Nakhsh-i-Rustám, which we shall describe bye and bye, we have, unquestionably, a native record of what the Persian ruler rightly deemed the chief glory of his reign. On these sculptures the position of the figures indicates the complete humbling of the Romans.

But a day of retribution was at hand. Odænathus, prince of Palmyra, whose magnificent presents Shahpúr had rejected with disdain in the hour of his triumph, collected a small army from the villages of

* Trebellius Pollio has preserved a haughty letter from Shahpúr to his allies and vassals, and the curious replies of three of them (Hist. August. Script.). In this war, the kings of Bactria, Albania (Georgia), and of Chersonesus Taurica, warned the Roman generals to keep their forces together, as, if so, they would join them against Shahpúr; but any advice recommending a spirited course of action would have failed of recognition by such a ruler as Gallienus.

Syria and the tents of the desert, and attacking the Persian army, laden with booty from the sack of Cæsarea, routed it in several engagements, and followed it nearly to the walls of Ctesiphon. "By this exploit," says Gibbon, "Odænathus laid the foundation of his future fame and fortunes. The majesty of Rome, oppressed by a Persian, was protected by a Syrian or an Arab of Palmyra." The reigns of his immediate successors, Hormazd I. and Varahrán I., leave nothing worthy of record, except, perhaps, the destruction of Mani or Manes, the celebrated founder of the Manichæan heresy, by the zealous followers of Zoroaster. The religion of which Mani professed himself the founder, if not the inspired prophet, appears to have been a mixture of the Hindú doctrine of metempsychosis, of the principles of good and evil, and of Christianity. He was fond of claiming for himself the name of Paraclete, and of asserting that he was the promised "Comforter."

In the reign of the second Varahrán, the Roman arms were successful under Carus, who, rejecting the offers of the Persian ambassadors, crossed with his victorious forces the whole of Mesopotamia, and (in this superior, alike, to Trajan and Severus) captured both Seleucia and Ctesiphon; nor would he have probably stayed his hand till all Persia was at his feet, had his career not been arrested by a thunder-storm, in or by which he himself lost his life. Gibbon (from Synesius) gives a picturesque story of the visit of Persian ambassadors to the Roman camp, and tells us how they found the old emperor seated on the grass, scarcely distinguishable by a richer dress from the soldiers around him, with his supper before him of a piece of stale bacon and a few hard peas. Taking off a cap he wore to cover or conceal his baldness, the Roman emperor bid them assure their master that unless he at once acknowledged the superiority of Rome " he would render Persia as naked of trees as his own head was destitute of hair."*

Somewhat later, in the reign of Narses, a war of greater and more important dimensions took place, some details of which must be given, as throwing considerable light on the policy of the Roman and Persian leaders respectively. We have already stated that the Persians were ever anxious to secure either the actual possession of the adjoining province of Armenia, or to be at least on friendly terms with it, the Romans, on the other hand, being equally desirous of aiding the native tribes as a set off against the constant hostility of the Persians. Thus, during the reign of Valerian, Armenia had been seized by the Persians, and its monarch slain; his youthful son, however, Tiridates, escaped to Rome, where, acquiring many arts he could not have learned in Armenia, he soon showed himself worthy of his teachers. Of great courage and personal strength, even Olympia recognized him a victor in one of its games. But Tiridates was more than a mere soldier; he was grateful to those with whom he had passed his long exile; moreover, Licinius, the intimate

* See also Vopiscus, ap. Hist. August. Script.

friend and constant companion of Galerius, owed his life to the personal prowess of Tiridates: hence, when Galerius was associated in the empire by Diocletian, the investiture of the distinguished Armenian, as the restored king of his native land, was an act as natural as it was wise.

On his return to Armenia, Tiridates was universally received with the greatest joy, the rule of the Persians during the previous twenty-six years having been marked by the tyranny the usual accompaniment of their government. Thus, though they erected many buildings of splendor, the money for them had been wrung from the hard hands of the Armenian peasantry; the religion of Zoroaster had been rigorously enforced, and the statues of the deified kings of Armenia, with the sacred images of the sun and moon, had been broken in pieces by the conquerors. At first, all went well with Tiridates, and he expelled the aggressive Persians from Armenia; but here his career was arrested, and the restored king of Armenia, though a soldier of renown, had, after the loss of a great battle, to take refuge for a second time with his Roman friends, involving as this did, almost necessarily, a new war with Persia, to avenge alike the wrongs of Tiridates and the injured majesty of Rome.

To direct the whole force of the empire against the Persian ruler, Diocletian himself took up his abode at Antioch, while the command of the legions was given to the intrepid Galerius, for this purpose summoned from the banks of the Danube. But his former bravery did not here avail him, not impossibly because the troops he had with him were of an inferior quality, a force gathered chiefly from the enervated denizens of the oriental towns or from the yet more unwarlike natives of Asia Minor. In the third, it would seem, of three battles, the army of Galerius, worn out by the heat and want of water, was surrounded and destroyed by the Persians in the great plain below Carrhæ, on nearly the same ground which had before witnessed the death of Crassus and the overthrow of his legions. Tiridates, after fighting to the last, saved his life by swimming the Euphrates, and Galerius, in great disgrace, returned to Diocletian. Nor did he escape without a public chastisement of his misfortune. "The haughtiest of men," says Gibbon, "clothed in his purple, but humbled by the sense of his fault and misfortunes, was obliged to follow the emperor's chariot above a mile on foot, and to exhibit before the whole Court the spectacle of his disgrace."

But neither Diocletian nor Galerius were men to remain long quiet under unavenged wrongs. An army having been rapidly collected, this time from the tried veterans of Illyria, aided by Gothic auxiliaries in Imperial pay, Galerius again crossed the Euphrates, and, avoiding the heats of the plain countries by clinging to the friendly mountains of Armenia, secured, in this way, ground especially favorable for his most important arm, his infantry. His plans were crowned with success. A night attack, generally fatal as these are to Eastern forces, surprised the Persians with their horses tied up, and ended in the total defeat of Narses. All his baggage, including his wives and children, fell into the hands of the Roman general, who, emulating the example of Alexander, treated them with the respect due to their age, sex, and dignity.

The result was a conference between the emperors and the Persian ambassador at Nisibis, with the view of arranging a treaty which it was hoped would secure peace for a long time. Both sides were indeed weary of war: Diocletian was only anxious to preserve the limits of the Roman empire, as suggested by Augustus and acted on by Hadrian, while the Persian ambassador pointed out that the Roman and Persian empires were the two "eyes of the world," which would remain imperfect and mutilated, if either of them was put out. The treaty, at length signed, ceded to Rome Mesopotamia and the mountains of the Carduchi (now Kurdistán), with the right to nominate the kings of Iberia; while, at the same time the boundaries of the kingdom of Armenia were restored and enlarged. The acknowledged equity of the grounds on which this treaty rested, secured a peace of forty years for the Eastern empire, and, at the close of the war, Diocletian and Maximian celebrated at Rome their successes and those of their lieutenants, by a triumph, the last that Rome ever witnessed. Indeed, as Gibbon justly remarks, "soon after this time, the emperors ceased to vanquish, and Rome ceased to be the capital of the empire."

Into the legendary history of the great ruler who followed, Shahpúr II. (A.D. 310-380), we need not enter, nor need we discuss the question whether the diadem he wore, much to his country's advantage, for the unusual period of seventy years, was actually prepared for him by a submissive nobility, while he was yet an unborn baby. They who care for such matters, may consult the Zeenat-al-Tuarikh, or Sir J. Malcolm's abridgement of it. Suffice it to say, that, when scarcely more than a boy, Shahpúr made strenuous resistance to the Greeks, Tátárs and Arabs, who, relying on his youth and inexperience, invaded his empire; thus showing, from the very first, the metal of which he was made. Collecting his forces, we are told, that he marched against the Arabs, drove them out of his country, and chasing them across the Arabian desert to Yathreb, massacred every one he met. From the peculiar punishment he invented to create terror among these wild tribes, he obtained his distinguishing name of Zu'-laktaf, or "Lord of the shoulders."* From Hedjáz he carried his arms into Syria, and turning northward, swept the whole country to the gates of Aleppo ere he returned to Ctesiphon. The presence

* Mirkhond says he was only sixteen, and that, in this war, he completely secured all the lower end of Babylonia and crossing the sea by Al Cathif, put to the sword many of the people of Bahrein and Hedjáz and of the tribe of Temin. It is clear, therefore, that St. Martin was wrong in supposing that the Sassanians did not conquer Mesene till A.D. 389. As we shall see this date (A.D. 326) agrees well with the narrative in Ammianus of the fatal march of Julian thirty-seven years later.

of such a foe awakened the fast declining spirit of the Romans, yet, during the later days of the reign of Constantine the prudence of Shahpúr prevented an open rupture.

With the death of Constantine matters changed, and the despot of the East conceived himself bound to repress the despot of the West. Five provinces had been ceded to Rome after the peace of Galerius, and these he felt it his duty to recover, by treaty, if possible; if not, by force of arms. The disturbed state of the Western Empire favored his views; the legions were corrupt and lacked the firm grasp of the veteran emperor; the great Tiridates, after a reign of fifty-six years, was no more, though, by becoming a Christian shortly before his death, he had strengthened the link that bound Armenia to Constantinople. Still a large faction remained in Armenia who, misliking the change of life Christianity demanded, were ready to aid Shahpúr, though with the certain suppression of their own political independence. Hence, the might of Shahpúr, soon overcame Chosroes, the puny successor of Tiridates, and hence, too, the siege by the Persian of Nisibis and his occupation of great part of Mesopotamia. Yet it must not be supposed that the Romans tamely succumbed to the rising power of the Persians. So far from it, it is clear that the son and successor of Constantine, Constantius, did his best to secure the frontier of his empire from the incessant inroads of their light horse. Details in these matters are wanting, and accounts vary; but it seems certain that, of nine bloody fields, in two of which Constantius commanded in person, the general result was in favor of the Persian.

Of these, the most memorable was the battle of Singara, in which, as long as daylight lasted, the Persians failed to hold their own against the Roman veterans, who forced their camp: but the following night told a different tale. In the silence of that night, Shahpúr drew together his forces, many of which had been watching the action of the previous day on secure heights, and falling on the Roman troops, dispersed here and there and rejoicing in the plunder of the Persian camp, cut them to pieces, with an incredible slaughter. The end therefore, of the battle of Singara, though it was victorious at its commencement, was the entire rout and destruction of the army of Constantius. Yet the Persian, superior in the plain, where he had ample room to manœuvre his chief arm, cavalry, failed as surely when he had to besiege a fortified town; hence he was forced to raise the siege of Nisibis, with a loss, it is said, of 20,000 men. Moreover, as he was, about the same time, invaded from the North by the Massagetæ, he thought it as well to patch up a hasty peace with Constantius, who, at the same time, was nothing loath to do so, as, by the death of his two brothers, he was involved in a civil contest demanding the utmost exertion of his undivided strength. The rulers of the East and the West, were, as it happened, at almost the same time, though at a distance of more than two thousand miles, engaged in repelling, as best they could, the impetuous onslaught of the barbarians of the North. If Shahpúr had his Massagetæ to deal with, Constantius found an equal foe in the Sarmatians.

At the conclusion of these two wars, an attempt to establish a treaty between the rival emperors, which Constantius seems to have been really anxious to effect, was frustrated by an adventurer named Antoninus, and Shahpúr, unfolding his standards, crossed the head waters of the Euphrates in another invasion of Asia Minor. Finding most of the fortified towns well prepared to resist him, he wisely, for a time, kept aloof from needless sieges, yet was he tempted, in a moment of rashness, to attempt that of Amida, and, though successful, lost the flower of his army, indeed, if the historians of the time can be credited, so large a number as 30,000 men. In fact, the actual result of a campaign, which was to have suppressed the Roman power in the East, was limited to the reduction of the two fortified towns of Singara and Bezabde. Nor indeed did the late return of Constantius himself to the scene do any thing towards redeeming the waning reputation of Rome; especially as he failed with disgrace to recover the captured Bezabde, though its walls were repeatedly shaken by the most powerful battering rams then available. But Shahpúr was now too opposed by a new emperor; who, had he had knowledge comparable with his energy, might have won back for Rome nearly all she had lost. In Julian, many hoped, perhaps some thought, the best times of Rome were returning, and Shahpúr at once made overtures of peace to him, but in vain.

Of this strange genius, yet most remarkable man, we have not space to say much; but this is clear, that, to a mind deeply devoted to the philosophic fancies of his age, he added the most burning desire to distinguish himself as a military leader. Indeed, he seems to have felt himself a second Alexander. "The successor of Cyrus and of Artaxerxes," says Gibbon, "was the only rival he had deemed worthy of his arms, and he resolved by a final conquest of Persia, to chastise the haughty nation, which had so long resisted and insulted the majesty of Rome." In his "Cæsares," Julian himself remarks, "Alexander reminds his rival, Cæsar, who depreciated the fame and the merit of an Asiatic victory, that Crassus and Antony had felt the Persian arrows; and that the Romans, in a war of three hundred years, had not yet subdued a single province of Mesopotamia or Assyria."

But, except in zeal, and we are bound to add, in personal courage, Julian altogether lacked the ability for carrying out the schemes he had proposed to himself, while he had to deal with a population corrupted by wealth and luxury, and was himself, from his change of religion, inimical to many whom he might otherwise have conciliated. It is certain too, that Julian had, by a strange want of judgment, greatly alienated the affections of those on whom he had chiefly to rely. Thus at Antioch, we learn that, during a season of scarcity, he adopted the dangerous plan of fixing by authority, the value of corn, and when this corn was bought up, as it was sure to be by a few wealthy speculators, consigned to prison the whole of the senators of that city, 200 in number. It is no matter of surprise, therefore, that with such causes of dissension at home, Julian was worse than usually prepared to attack such an enemy as he who then held the sceptre of the Persians. Early in March A.D. 363, Julian took the field from Antioch, and passing Berrhœa and Hierapolis, advanced at once to Carrhæ, the neighborhood of which had been already fatal to two Roman armies. There, with a singular want of generalship dividing his army, he left Procopius to secure the upper waters of the Tigris, while he himself took the line of the Euphrates; a plan, which, for its success, depended much on the support of the king of Armenia, who, it is said, was not over-pleased with some injudicious letters he had received from Julian.

Following the course of the Euphrates, Julian arrived in a month at Circesium (Carchemish), the extreme limit of the Roman dominions, one division of his army being under the command of a certain Hormazd, who, though of the royal blood of Persia, had from early youth attached himself to the cause of the Romans. In his advance Julian seems to have met with little serious resistance, the inhabitants of the open towns, for the most part, taking to flight; his rear and flanks, however, suffered incessant annoyance from clouds of mounted Arabs, in the pay of Persia, who lost no opportunity of harassing his troops. "The fields of Assyria," says Gibbon, "were devoted by Julian to the calamities of war; and the philosopher retaliated on a guiltless people the acts of rapine and cruelty, which had been committed by their haughty master in the Roman provinces. The trembling Assyrians summoned the rivers to their assistance, and completed with their own hands the ruin of their country."

But the Romans struggled on, and with undaunted perseverance overcame every obstacle; Perisabor and Maozamalcha were taken by hard fighting; and Julian exclaimed with natural pride, "We have now provided some materials for the sophist of Antioch" (Libanius). In a few days more, the passage of the Tigris was forced, and the Persians driven under the walls of Ctesiphon. But here, Julian's real difficulties began; indeed each Mesopotamian campaign seems to repeat the previous one. The defection of the king of Armenia and his own incapacity had prevented Procopius from joining the Emperor, by a parallel march along the Tigris, and Julian was forced, though most reluctantly, to give up the siege of the great capital of Shahpúr; at the same time, rashly burning his boats and fancying himself another Alexander, he advanced like a madman, in pursuit of the still retreating enemy, giving willing heed to every idle tale he could pick up from the Persian deserters of the terror his onward march inspired. The fate of the Roman army was not long deferred; the Persians gradually closed round them; food was scarce, and the heat intolerable to the hardy warriors of Germany and Gaul; till, at length, having lost thousands of his best troops, Julian was himself slain, after a brief but remarkable reign of a year and eight months.* His successor, Jovian, accepted terms of peace few Roman leaders would have acknowledged. The five provinces beyond the Tigris, ceded by the grandfather of Shahpúr, were restored by him; Nisibis and Singara given up; while a special article required the abandonment for ever by the Romans of the kingdom of Armenia. "The predecessors of Jovian," adds Gibbon, "had sometimes relinquished the dominion of distant and unprofitable provinces; but since the foundation of the city, the genius of Rome, the god Terminus who guarded the boundaries of the Republic, had never retired before the sword of a victorious enemy." In fact, the treaty assented to by Jovian, gave up nearly all that the victories of Galerius had secured.

Little is known of the history of Shahpúr after the

* Ammianus gives an interesting account of the state of the country through which Julian marched, and is mainly supported by the narratives of Magnus of Charræ, and of Eutychianus of Cappadocia, who also accompanied Julian (see John Malala). These writers all speak of what they call the great canal of the Euphrates, and of the dams across the rivers, of which Layard gives such a vivid description. With Arrian, they call these dams *cataractæ*, a word which Yacút says is of Nabathæan origin. These dams were not to prevent, as Layard thinks, hostile shipping ascending the rivers, but rather to keep up a sufficient supply of water for irrigation. The great canal is doubtless the *Nahar-al-malk* which, according to Abydenus, was made by Nebuchadnezzar. The Greek *Armacal* is, I supect, but a transposition of the letters of the previous word.

conclusion of the Roman war, but he is said to have contended with doubtful fortune for the possession of Armenia, and to have made a fresh irruption into the Roman dominions. Finally, in the reign of Gratian, he ended his long and glorious reign of fully seventy years.

His two immediate successors, Ardashír II. and Shahpúr III., did nothing worthy of commemoration; nor is the third one in succession, Varahrán IV., famous for anything except as the founder of the city of Kirmanshah, and the part-executor of the famous sculptures of Takt-i-Bostán, five miles from it. The inscriptions still remaining there, first deciphered by De Sacy, leave no doubt that they were chiefly made by his order, to perpetuate his own name and the glory of Shahpúr II.

The rule of the next emperor, Jezdigird, is variously related by the writers of the East and the West, the former speaking of him, as an implacable and worthless tyrant, the latter as a wise and virtuous prince. Perhaps the differing tenor of these reports is traceable to the fact that he lived on terms of friendship as well as of peace with the Roman Arcadius, who, at his death, declared him the protector of his son, Theodosius the Second. As the young man grew up, the ties of friendship were strengthened between the two empires, and the influence of the Bishop Marathas, the ablest of the ministers of Theodosius, was highly beneficial to the Christians, who had now become an important body in Persia. Hitherto they had been, with some reason, held to be bad subjects, their inclinations leading them to support the views of the Christian emperors of Constantinople; but, from this charge, the bishop, at least during his lifetime, seems to have successfully vindicated them. But Persian toleration was rarely of long endurance. In the next reign, that of Varahrán V,* a fierce persecution broke out, though the king himself inclined to mercy; and the then Christian prelate having imprudently burnt one of the fire temples, the rage of the populace could not be restrained, and the bishop and a large number of the Christians were put to death with great cruelty. The natural result of these excesses was a fresh war between the Romans and the Persians, prolonged with various success: as, however, the Persians on the whole had suffered the most, they were willing to accept terms of peace, to which they would hardly otherwise have assented.

About the year A.D. 458, Firúz I., ascended the throne, and was soon engaged in a memorable war with the Huns, which, after lasting for several years and entailing heavy losses on the Persians, was finally terminated by his own death and the destruction of his army. It was during the latter years of the reign of Kobád, and after a series of conflicts

* The Oriental writers assert that Varahrán V. made a voyage to India about A.D. 435, and married an Indian princess. If the story be true, it is most likely that India means Beluchistán, or else the country at the mouth of the Indus. Varahrán V. is sometimes called *Gaur*, from his enthusiastic passion for hunting the *Gaur*, or wild ass.

M

between the East and the West, so alike in character and result, as to be wearisome in their description, that the Romans, to prevent the constant inroads of the Persians, founded a new colony at Dara, about fourteen miles from Nisibis, with walls of such strength as to be impregnable to any machines of war their enemies could bring against them. "Dara continued more than sixty years," says Gibbon, "to fulfil the wishes of its founders, and to provoke the jealousy of the Persians, who incessantly complained that this impregnable fortress had been constructed in manifest violation of the treaty of peace between the two empires."

At length, in A.D. 531, Khosrú Nushírwán* was chosen emperor, becoming thus the contemporary of the great law-maker, Justinian. Nushírwán is still the synonym in the mouth of every Persian for wisdom, justice and munificence, and could we forget his constant perfidy, an evil quality about which his subjects are not supposed to have cared much, he well deserved a reputation, which even partial historians have not perhaps rated too highly. He found his empire groaning under every kind of abuse, among the worst being the prevalence of a sect, who, under their leader Mazdac, held the doctrine of community of women, with other practices

* Abundant myths have grown up around the name of Nushírwán. A proposal is said to have been made in his youth, that he should be adopted by the Emperor Justin; and, that he was baptized as a Christian a little before his death, is another story about which there is more than doubt.

which, in recent years, have made Mormonism intolerable, even in the far West. From the evil results of the doctrines promulgated by this vagabond, Nushírwán gradually relieved his subjects, rooting out the delusion by the simple process of destroying the prophet and his followers. He then restored the bridges, rebuilt towns and villages which had fallen into decay, and held out such encouragement to men of learning, that even the philosophers of Greece flocked to his Court. The literature of Greece and Rome were collected by his diligence; Aristotle and Plato translated into Persian; and portions of what we now know to have been originally in Sanskrit, as the so-called " Fables of Pilpay," or "Hito-padésa," were brought from India.

In his first war with Justinian, Nushírwán maintained his superiority by the extortion from the humbled emperor of eleven thousand pounds of gold,* as the price of a perpetual peace! and, in his later reduction of Antioch and Syria (A.D. 540), and in the extension of the Persian territories from the banks of the Phasis to the Mediterranean, and from the Red Sea to the Oxus and Jaxartes, we see abundant proof of his military genius, or of the weakness of the Romans. One great general alone withstood his further progress, and the veteran Belisarius, recalled from his Western victories, twice arrested his onward advance; thus achieving a success which,

* The peace so disgracefully purchased from the 'Persians, enabled Justinian to carry on his wars with the West, and to reduce Carthage, Sicily, and Italy.

considering the scant means at his disposal and the character of the Court he served, must be considered remarkable.

In all the negotiations which took place between Justinian and Nushírwán, the latter invariably assumed the tone of a superior, nor, though his reign extended to nearly forty-eight years, and his life to more than eighty, do we find his head turned by this unusual prosperity. The firmness of his character enabled him to resist the influence of the luxury by which he was surrounded; he neither gave himself up to it, nor permitted it in others; indeed, but little before his death, the aged monarch led in person his troops to the attack on Dara (A.D. 573), with a spirit as active and as daring as he had shown in his earliest enterprises. The last days, however, of his life, were marked by some failures, the Emperor Justin having yielded to the importunities of the Turks, who offered an alliance against the common enemy; and, in the battle of Melitene, the Scythian chief turned the flank of the Persians, attacked their rear-guard, in the presence of Nushírwán himself, and pillaged his camp. The Romans, too, on their side, were left masters of the field, and their general Justinian, after attacking Dara, was permitted to erect his standard on the shores of the Caspian. This inland sea was now, for the first time, explored by a hostile fleet, and seventy thousand captives transplanted from the shores of Hyrcania to the Island of Cyprus.

The reign of Nushírwán's successor, Hormazd, is

chiefly remarkable for the gallant conduct of a rebel chief, who bore the time-honored name of Varahrán. Hormazd had allowed his father's empire to fall into decay; all the outlying provinces, Babylon, Susa, Caramania, Arabia, India and Scythia, were in revolt; and the Romans, taking advantage of these dissensions, had made constant inroads into Mesopotamia and Assyria.

But "Persia lost by a king, was saved by a hero." Varahrán, known before for his valor at the siege of Dara, repelled the Tátár host near the Caspian gates, but was less successful, when shortly afterwards he was attacked by the veteran troops of Rome, under the command of Romanus, the lieutenant of the emperor Mauricius. Having on this occasion received an insulting message from Hormazd, he threw off his allegiance, with the ready assent of his troops and of the people generally, to whom that ruler had made himself hateful. A revolution, however, broke out at Ctesiphon, and the son of Hormazd, Khosrú II. (Parviz), ascended his father's throne (A.D. 591): but in conflict with Varahrán, he was hopelessly beaten, and condemned to take refuge within the dominions of Mauricius, who readily espoused his cause.

A powerful army was shortly after (A.D. 591) assembled on the frontiers of Syria and Armenia, under the command of the best general of his time, Narses, with orders not to sheath the sword, till Khosrú was replaced on the throne of his ancestors. "The restoration of Khosrú was celebrated with feasts and executions, and the music of the royal banquet was often disturbed by the groans of dying or mutilated criminals."

During the reign of Mauricius, the Persian ruler was not forgetful of the power to whom he owed his throne; the cities of Martyropolis and of Dara were restored to the Romans, the banks of the Araxes and the shores of the Caspian forming the boundaries of their empire. But these advantages were not destined to remain for many years under the command of the feeble Constantinopolitans, the murder of Mauricius and of his family by the upstart Phocas producing such a revolution as might easily have been foreseen. When Khosrú heard of this murder he instantly declared war (nominally at least) to avenge the death of his benefactor, and doubtless, at first, owed much of his success to the destruction of the unfortunate Narses, who had been seized by Phocas, and burnt alive in the market-place of Constantinople (A.D. 605). Indeed, during the short reign of this usurper, the Persians were everywhere victorious: "the fortifications of Mardin, Dara, Amida, and Edessa," says Gibbon, "were besieged, reduced or destroyed by the Persian monarch; he passed the Euphrates, occupied the Syrian cities Hierapolis and Berrhæa or Aleppo, and soon emcompassed the walls of Antioch, with his irresistible arms . . . . . . The first intelligence from the East, which Heraclius (the successor of Phocas) received, was that of the loss of Antioch: but the ancient metropolis, so often overturned by earthquakes, or pillaged by an enemy, could supply but a small and languid stream of treasure and blood. The Persians were equally successful, and more fortunate in the sack of Cæsarea, the capital of Cappadocia, and, as they advanced beyond the ramparts of the frontiers, the boundary of ancient war, they found a less obstinate resistance and a more plentiful harvest . . . . . . The conquest of Jerusalem, which had been meditated by Nushírwán, was achieved by the zeal of his grandson . . . . . . The sepulchre of Christ, and the stately churches of Helena and Constantine were consumed, or at least damaged by the flames; the devout offerings of three hundred years were rifled in one sacrilegious day. Egypt itself, the only province which had been exempt since the time of Diocletian from foreign and domestic war, was again subdued by the successors of Cyrus. Pelusium, the key of that impervious country, was surprised by the cavalry of the Persians . . . . . . and Chosroes entered the second city of the empire (Alexandria), which still retained a wealthy remnant of industry and commerce . . . . . . In the first campaign, another army advanced from the Euphrates to the Thracian Bosphorus; Chalcedon surrendered after a long siege, and a Persian camp was maintained for ten years in the presence of Constantinople. The sea coast of Pontus, the city of Ancyra, and the Island of Rhodes, are enumerated among the latest conquests (A.D. 620) of the great king, and if Chosroes had possessed any maritime power, his boundless ambition would have spread slavery and desolation over the provinces of Europe."

It is impossible not to see, in this long career of victory and plunder, that the Persian ruler was really consulting his own tastes and that of his people, rather than avenging the memory of Mauricius, else, on the death of Phocas, he would have made friends with Heraclius, who had already sufficiently punished those who had been the chief agents in the fate of his predecessor. On the contrary, Khosrú rejected, with disdain, the repeated embassies of Heraclius, entreating him to spare the innocent, to accept a tribute, and thus to give peace to the world. When, on the treachery of the Avars, Heraclius was compelled to fly from his capital, the Persian lieutenant of Khosrú at Chalcedon, pitying his fate, offered to send an embassy for aid to his master. "It was not an embassy," replied the tyrant of Asia, "it was the person of Heraclius bound in chains, that he should have brought to the foot of my throne. I will never give peace to the emperor of Rome, till he has abjured his crucified God, and embraced the worship of the Sun."

But a retribution soon followed, little anticipated from the previous character and conduct of the Greek emperor. The war that had found Heraclius the slave of sloth and pleasure, aroused the spirit of a hero. "The Arcadius of the palace arose the Cæsar of the camp;" and the honor of Rome and of Heraclius was gloriously retrieved by the exploits and trophies of six adventurous campaigns. The sun indeed of the Sassanians had now well-nigh set. A campaign of great brilliancy restored the provinces of Asia Minor, and the hard-fought battle of Issus the losses of many previous years. Pursuing his march, Heraclius crossed the heights of Taurus, and sweeping the plains of Cappadocia, went into winter quarters on the banks of the Halys. The following year saw this second Hannibal exploring his perilous way through the mountains of Armenia, and advancing almost on the footsteps of Antony to Ganzaca, the ancient capital of Media Atropatene; the ruin of Urmíah, one of the traditional birthplaces of Zoroaster, in some degree atoning for the spoil of the Holy Sepulchre. Another campaign carried the arms of the Romans to the neighborhood of Kashán and Ispahán, which had never yet been approached by a Western conqueror.

Alarmed at the successes of Heraclius, Khosrú recalled his forces from the Nile and the Bosphorus and three formidable armies surrounded the camp of the emperor. But the danger was met by a general equal to the occasion. "Be not dismayed," exclaimed the intrepid Heraclius, "with the aid of heaven one Roman may triumph over a horde of barbarians. If we devote our lives for the salvation of our brethren we shall obtain the crown of martyrdom, and our immortal reward will be liberally paid by God and posterity." The victory which ensued was the reply to his prayers, and Heraclius returned in triumph to Constantinople with the recovery of three hundred Roman standards and the deliverance of innumerable captives from the prisons of Edessa and Alexandria. The reign of Khosrú terminated after thirty-eight years by his murder: had it been six years shorter it would have been one of unbroken success. Historians are not agreed as to the personal share Khosrú had in his earlier and glorious wars, and some, like Malcolm, attribute all his gains to the ability of his generals. This much, however, is certain that the later victories of Heraclius nearly annihilated his former power, and practically destroyed the rule of the Sassanian house.

But a new era was now about to commence for the nations of the East and a revolution to take place, which has impressed a lasting character on a large section of mankind. Muhammed, who was born during the reign of Nushírwán, had been zealously preaching his new religion, and a willing army was now ready to enforce doctrines so acceptable to most of those to whom they were addressed. The religion of Muhammed, though containing in it some noble and sublime views, directly borrowed from the Bible, exhibited from its very origin the character of violence. The goods of this world and every earthly enjoyment were the pious prizes of the faithful soldier who drew his sword against the enemies of Muhammed: moreover, if he fell in this glorious career, a paradise was open for his reception, with all the pleasures of the senses at his fullest and freest disposal. Nor indeed has Muhammedanism even now lost its aggressive character. Dr. Barth relates, how, in the centre of Africa, he found a religious war in full force, the object being to compel the fetish-worshiping Africans to embrace its tenets.

Some years before the war with Heraclius, Khosrú had received a letter from the "camel-driver of Mecca," enjoining him to abjure the faith of his ancestors, and to embrace the worship of the "One True God," of Whom he, Muhammed, professed himself the Apostle. The indignant monarch, tearing the letter in pieces, cast the fragments into the Karasú, by the side of which he was then encamped. To this action, Muhammedan writers attribute all the subsequent misfortunes of this prince; nor, indeed, has this belief even now faded away. Malcolm, when himself halting at this river, in 1800, remarked to a Persian that its banks were very high, and its waters, therefore, of comparatively little use for the purposes of irrigation. "It once fertilized the whole country," replied the zealous Muhammedan, "but its channel sank with horror from its banks when that madman, Khosrú, threw our holy prophet's letter into the stream; which has ever since been accursed and useless."

The first attacks of the Arabs were repelled; but the Khalif Omar continually supplying fresh reinforcements, the battle of Kadesiah well retrieved their former disasters; and the glory of Persia, as an independent country, ceased forever, when the famous Darafsh-i-Kawáni was captured by the Arabs. The sack of Madain (Ctesiphon), and the carnage of Nehavend followed, and the empire of the Sassanidæ and with it the religion of Zoroaster, as a national faith, fell from the grasp of Yezdigird III., the last feeble ruler of this house. Thus ended, in

A.D. 641, a dynasty who had ruled Persia for 415 years, and which in the hands of Ardashír I., Shahpúr II., Nushírwán and Khosrú II., had extended its glories from the sands of Libya to the waters of the Indus.

It now only remains for me to notice briefly some of the remarkable monuments of Sassanian times still remaining in Persia, attesting as these do the power of the great monarchs by whom they were executed; and I will take first those of Nakhsh-i-Rustám, the place famous, as already noticed, for the tomb of Darius. From Sir R. K. Porter we learn that there are here three figures; of whom the two leaders are engaged in grasping, with outstretched arms, a wreath or twisted bandeau, from which hang a couple of waving ends. "'The first figure, which holds it in his right hand, stands on the right of the sculpture, and appears to be a king. He is crowned with a diadem of a bonnet shape, round which runs a range of upward fluted ornaments with a balloon-like mass rising from the middle of the crown* . . . . His hair is full, flowing, and curled, having nothing of the stiff wig appearance, so remarkable in the bas-reliefs of the Achæmenian period. The beard of this figure is very singularly disposed. On the upper lip, it is formed

---

*This head-dress is the same as may be seen on a large number of the coins of the Sassanian dynasty; it is still represented, though shorn of its pearls and precious stones, in the high cap worn by the Parsees of Bombay. The coins exhibit several different varieties of this head-dress.

like moustachios, and grows from the front of the ear, down the whole of the jaw, in neat, short curls, but on the chin it becomes of great length (which, as I have observed before, seems to be the lasting attribute of royalty in Persia), and is tied together, just at the point of the chin, whence it hangs like a large tassel* . . . . His tunic has tight long sleeves, and is bound by a belt which passes over the right hip; the folds of the tunic at the top of the belt are well expressed in the stone. To the other side of this girdle it is probable the sword is attached, the hilt of which he is grasping with his left hand. On my arrival afterwards at Shiráz, a Persian artist showed me a very old drawing of this bas-relief, where the present mutilated space was filled by the upper part of the figure of a boy, crowned with a diadem like the personage on the left, and like the figure of the king, clasping the hilt of his sword with his left hand." Opposite to the king stands a figure whose closely fitting dress suggests a feminine form. A third figure with a short bushy beard stands behind the king. The composition of the piece seems to indicate a royal union, and may refer to Varahrán V., and his queen, who, besides being the partner of his domestic pleasures, was, as we may see from the coins of the period, associated with him and his son in the empire.

* Sir R. K. Porter had not, of course, seen the monuments discovered at Nimrúd and elsewhere by Mr. Layard and other excavators. The treatment of the beard would seem to have arrived at its culminating point of care and completeness as early as the ninth century B.C.

The next relief, a few paces from the former, represents a combat between two horsemen, and has been designed with much spirit. The chief figure, in the act of charging his opponent with a spear, exhibits considerable grace and harmony of action. He wears a winged helmet and scaly armor, not altogether unlike that of the Knights Templars. A second and prostrate figure lies under the belly of the horse of the principal one. A third relief in a more perfect state, consists of four figures, the chief one of which can hardly be any one but Shahpúr I. Before him is another figure, in the usual dress of a Roman soldier, with his arms extended as though seeking mercy, and his left knee bent. There is no reason to doubt that we have here the well-known story of the humbling of the Roman emperor Valerian by Shahpúr I., and it is the more interesting as the work is clearly that of a Persian artist. It has long since been suggested that the third figure to whom Shahpúr is giving his hand is Cyriades, the wretched nobody he is said to have placed on the throne.* The scale of this stone picture is colossal, the whole of the face of the rock having been excavated, and a tablet formed thirty-seven feet long, the horse alone occupying fourteen.

On a fourth sculpture is a repetition of the combat between Varahrán V., (Gaur) and a figure whom

---

* This portion of the story is represented elsewhere with slight differences. At Darabjerd, Shahpúr is placing his left hand on the head of Cyriades (Flandin, Pl. 31-33); at Shahpúr a single figure kneels before the conqueror's horse. (Flandin, Pl. 48.)

Sir R. Porter calls a Tátár prince. Though mutilated, it is in some respects better preserved than the former, and has some interest from the fact that over the whole of one of the figures are indications of a once perfect coat of small plate mail, the special dress, according to Heliodorus, of the cataphracti or heavy cavalry. The long pike, as noticed by the same writer, resembling those on the Achæmenian sculptures at Persepolis.

The fifth sculpture has peculiar excellence; and represents two men on horseback meeting, the one bestowing, the other receiving, the circlet or badge of sovereignty.* On the breast of the horses, just above their shoulders, are inscriptions in Greek and Pehlevi. The length of the excavation is twenty-one feet; and the monument is in white marble, its surface being polished and still well preserved. The general sense of the inscriptions confirms the attribution of one of the figures to Ardashír and of the other to Ormazd or (as De Sacy calls him) Jupiter.

The next sculptures to be noticed are those of Nakhsh-i-Regib, a portion of the Persepolitan range.

* Mr. Edward Thomas, F. R. S., who has studied the details of these monuments with great care (Asiat. Journal, 1868), thinks this subject is the bestowal by Ormazd of the imperial cydaris on Ardáshír Babekán for his victory over the last Arsakes, whose prostrate form is identified by the snake-crested Median helmet he wears, and his view is confirmed by the attached inscriptions. (Ker Porter, i. Pl. 23. Flandin, iv. pl. 182.) There is another sculpture at Nakhsh-i-Rustám, of the time of Narses, perhaps representing a similar investiture. This inscription is given, but incorrectly, by Morier, Pl. xxix. 1812. See however Flandin, Pl. 45, relief B, and Sculpt. Pl. 52, relief B.

Here a large natural recess is visible, enclosing sculptures evidently representing historical events. The one to the right is the same in subject, but smaller in dimensions, than that at Nakhsh-i-Rustám, and exhibits two horsemen holding between them the royal circlet;* its style, however, suggests a later age and less skilful workmen. It has moreover been greatly mutilated, probably as Chardin asserts, by the minister of the son of Shah Abbás, the marks of savage violence being but too visible. The next slab occupies the centre of the recess, and repeats the same subject, only that, on this occasion, the actors are on foot. This sculpture is unquestionably cœval with those at Nakhsh-i-Rustám. The third relief is the largest, and probably the most important. The leading personage on horseback, behind whom are nine followers, is evidently the king, and the whole most likely represents one of the many royal progresses. The king wears a dress of silk, or of some fine texture, falling over him lightly.† The attendants wear Margian helmets of steel, an excellent specimen of which, procured by Mr. Layard, and studded with golden nails, may be seen in the British Museum. On the inscription, Shahpúr is called "King of kings, king of Irán and Anirán."

* This sculpture seems to have been first noticed by Sir W. Ouseley, but not to have been recognized by either Morier or Ker Porter. It may, however, be seen in Flandin, Pl. 192, relief B.

† The same dress, chain armor over silk, may be seen on many Buddhistic figures, frequently brought to light by General Cunningham, and perhaps, too, on some of the Indo-Scythic coins.

Descending into the plain, Sir R. K. Porter found on the edge of the mountain a range of sculptures, belonging to the same period, but evidently never completed, as they are only blocked out. The most finished of them consists of two figures, one that of a woman, in light and delicate drapery, stretching out her right hand towards her companion, who wears the royal dress, common on the Sassanian reliefs. The remainder of the range comprises two more sculptures, both containing the effigies of the king, with the globular crown, a profusion of curls, a collar and ear-rings. Sir R. K. Porter notices also some sculptural remains of the same period at Rhey (Rhages), representing a horseman at full charge. In this case, though the rock has been smoothed away for a space of about sixteen by twelve feet, the sculpture has remained unfinished.

The ruins of Shahpúr, about fifteen miles north of Kazerún, are among the most celebrated works of Sassanian times, and yet, though but a few miles out of the road, they have been passed by every traveler from Tavernier and Thevenot down to Scott Waring: it was not, indeed, till Mr. Morier visited them in the year 1809, that anything was really known about them. Mr. Morier considers that the ruins of Shahpúr have extended over a circumference of about six miles, enclosing a tract of plain and a hill, on which the ancient citadel forms a conspicuous object. Mr. Morier describes the position as one of singular grandeur and beauty, and adds: "The first object which attracted our attention, was a mutilated sculpture of two colossal figures on horseback, carved on the upper superficies of the rock. The figure to the right was the most injured, the only part, indeed, that we could ascertain with precision, was one of the front, and two of the hinder feet of a horse, standing over the statue of a man, who was extended at his full length, his face turning outwardly, and reposed on his right hand, and his attire bearing marks of a Roman costume. A figure in the same dress * was placed in an attitude of supplication at the horse's knees, and a head in alto-relievo, just appeared behind the hinder feet . . . . . The next piece of sculpture (which, like the former, is carved upon the mountain of the citadel) is perfect in all its parts. It consists of three grand compartments; the central and most interesting representing a figure on horseback, whose dress announces a royal personage . . . . . . A quiver hangs by his side; in his right hand he holds the hand of a figure behind him, which stands so as to cover the whole hind-quarter of his horse, and is dressed in a Roman tunic and helmet. A figure, habited also in the Roman costume, is on its knees before the head of the horse, with its hands extended, and a face be-

* This is clearly another representation of the story of Valerian and Shahpúr: the figure kneeling may be Cyriades awaiting investiture; a subject more than once repeated with varying details. On another, but somewhat similar sculpture, the Roman emperor is not so readily recognized, and it is probable that this one refers to some other victory of the Persian monarch. It may be added that there is no trace in any of these reliefs, of any barbarous treatment of the emperor on the part of his captor.

traying entreaty. Under the feet of the horse is another figure extended, in the same attire and character as that of the other two Roman figures; to the right of the tablet stands a figure (behind that in a suppliant attitude) with his hands also extended, but dressed in a different manner, and, as far as we could judge, with features more Egyptian than European . . . . In another compartment are rows of people, apparently in the attitude of supplication, and in a third, rows of horsemen. The whole of this interesting monument is sculptured on a very hard rock, and still exhibits a fine polish. On the opposite side of the river is a long tablet containing a multitude of figures, the chief of whom is seated alone in a small compartment, with the sword between his legs, on the pommel of which he rests his hands." From the number, and variety of the figures represented to the right and the left (in one compartment a man is approaching carrying two heads), Mr. Morier, probably with justice, supposes the whole scene represents the king in his hall of audience, surrounded by his people, and perhaps by the representatives of the nations tributary to him. Further on Mr. Morier met with another sculpture, which he thus describes: "In the first row, at the top on the right, are a number of slight figures with their arms folded; the second is filled with a crowd, some of whom carry baskets; the third is equally covered; and in the right corner is a man conducting a lion by a chain. In the fourth, and just opposite the king, is a very remarkable group, whose loose and folded dresses denote Indians. One leads a horse, whose furniture I have drawn with some care, and behind the horse is an elephant. Under this and close to the ground are men in Roman costume; among them is a chariot, to which two horses are harnessed." On recrossing the river Mr. Morier discovered some splendidly built masonry, each stone four feet long, twenty-seven inches thick, and cut to the finest angles, the front, in fact, of a square building, the area of which is fifty-five feet. At the top there had been sphinxes couchant. Beyond this again were the remains of a small theatre.

It is natural that the chief subject of the sculptures at Shahpûr should be the overthrow of the emperor Valerian, as the city was in the heart of the ancient province of Persis. Indeed the province, of which it was a leading town, was their native seat, and contained their tombs, palaces, and treasures; moreover, when their empire was overthrown, it was still as a rule administered by its native princes. Here it is probable that the fire-worship was never wholly suppressed; indeed, so late as the tenth century, after 300 years of Muhammedanism, Ibn Haukal expressly observes that "no district or town of Fars was without a fire-temple." Shahpûr itself, like many other places in the East, suffered less from the first violence of the Arabian invasion than from the wars of the subsequent native dynasties: it gradually decayed, as have nearly all the sites of early Persian greatness. As late, however, as the sixteenth century, the name of Shahpúr occurs in a table of latitudes and longitudes attached to the Aín-i Akbari; its position is marked on a map of Cluverius in 1672; and D'Anville, on the authority of the Oriental writers, has so called a district of Persia.

Having now described the principal monuments of the south of Persia, we must, in conclusion, take a brief review of some in the northern part of the country, which are not less worthy of attentive notice and study; and we will take first those of Takht-i-Bostán, the throne of the gardens, a portion of the great rocky mass of Behistán. The rock itself is craggy, barren, and terrific; its towering heights frown darkly over the blooming vale of Kirmanshah, but, at the base of the mountain, bursts forth a stream of peculiar clearness, which the natives have named Shirín, in remembrance of the celebrated loves of Khosrú and the beautiful damsel of that name.

The monuments consist of two lofty and deep arches, excavated with great labor and skill on the face of the mountain; within which are several bas-reliefs, executed with remarkable spirit and excellence; while a little beyond, where the mountain recedes, a flight of several hundred steps is cut on the edge of the nearly precipitous cliffs, forming an intricate and dangerous ascent towards its summit, and finishing abruptly with an extensive ledge or platform.

On the edge of the river, Sir R. K. Porter noticed the remains of a statue of colossal size, now much mutilated, which he thinks must have fallen from the heights above; as on the ledge above is a row of sculptured feet broken off at the ankles. The largest arch measures in width twenty-four feet, and in depth twenty-one; and the face of the rock has been smoothed for a great distance above the sweep of the arch, and on each side. On the surface to the right and to the left are two upright entablatures, containing exquisitely carved ornamentation, adorned with foliage in a classical style. Above the keystone is a crescent, and at the end of each curve are gigantic female figures, resembling the usual type of Victory on Roman coins; the artists who carved them having been probably Greeks of Constantinople. The inner face of the excavation is divided into two compartments, the upper one of which contains three figures, viz., a female in the royal dress and wearing the Sassanian diadem; a central figure, doubtless the monarch himself; and a third one wearing a diadem like that on the female head, and engaged in presenting a diadem to the king. The lower space is almost wholly occupied by a colossal equestrian figure of Khosrú II., both horse and rider being covered with a coat of mail.* The whole character of the man and horse resembles very much the huge metal-covered knights to be seen in illuminated copies of Froissart's Chronicles. This sculpture has been much damaged by the Arabs, and there are no intelligible remains of the inscriptions once engraven on it. The details have, however,

---

*See Numismatic Chronicle, vol. XIII., coin No. 80.

been worked out with great care, and, with the groups above, afford accurate and valuable specimens of the royal and military costumes of the period.

The sides of the arch are covered with representations of the sports of the field, wild boar and stag hunts. Many of the persons are mounted, while boats also appear, probably to indicate a marshy country intersected by small lakes; from these, sportsmen are discharging their arrows; while ponderous elephants, with their riders, plunge through the bushes in every direction. Two of the boats are filled with harpers, perhaps women; in a third are men with pipes. In the centre of the scene is a boat, in which stands a personage in stature gigantically taller than any of the other figures, and a little lower in the line of the hunt is a second figure slightly smaller than the first, with a halo or saintly glory round his head. This figure is receiving an arrow from one of his attendants, and a woman sits near him in the same boat, playing on the harp. The bas-relief of the figure under the arch, as well as the similar figures on the coins, represent the women as unveiled, thus showing that they were not at that time as rigidly secluded as they have been since the enforcement of the Muhammedan religion.

On the opposite side of the arch is another relief, representing the chase of the deer. On this the chief personage appears nearly at the top of the sculpture, entering the field in state, under the shade of an umbrella, and mounted on a richly caparisoned horse. Below is a similar figure, but this time moving at full speed. Towards the top of the relief is raised a scaffold, on which rows of musicians are seated, playing on various instruments, all curious specimens of the art of the period. In another compartment we see the carrying off of the spoil, and elephants in pursuit of the deer. This bas-relief is finished in only a few places; parts are merely begun, but what has been completed, both in this, and on the opposite side, is executed in a masterly style. It has been supposed that the group of the three figures above the equestrian warrior, commemorates the double gift by the emperor Mauricius to the Persian king of his bride and his crown. On this supposition, Khosrú is standing in his robes of inauguration between the imperial pair, the princess on the one side holding a diadem, and the emperor on the other presenting the new king with the crown, to which the arms of the Romans had restored him. At the same time it must be remembered that it is purely an Oriental tradition which gives Khosrú a Greek wife, the daughter of his benefactor, Mauricius, and that the story is scarcely probable.

The second arch is smaller in its dimensions than the former, being only nine feet wide by twelve in depth. The figures on each side were originally rudely and carelessly sculptured, and are now still less visible owing to the wilful mutilation they have sustained. The monument, however, is of value from the inscriptions still remaining on it, which prove that one of the figures is meant for Shahpúr

II., (Zu'laktaf), another for his son Shahpúr III., and the third for Varahrán IV., (Kirmanshah), his brother.

I have already noticed that many of the Sassanian monuments bear inscriptions in Pehlevi, giving the names and titles of the personages represented. But there are two remarkable groups of inscriptions recently made known by the labors of Mr. Edward Thomas, the second of which, if correctly interpreted, reads like a new chapter in the history of the East. The first group is known by the name of the "Pai Kuli" inscriptions, and was copied by Sir H. C. Rawlinson and Mr. Alex. Hector, in 1844, from a large number of blocks of stone which had fallen down from a building originally placed on a rocky crag at no great distance from Suleimánieh. Only detached portions of one or more long inscriptions were recoverable, but Sir Henry Rawlinson thinks there is as much more left behind to reward any future traveler who may have the means of raising the fallen blocks. On these are found the names of Ardashír Babekán, Tiridates, of Jews, and, perhaps, of Surena, together with those of Persia, Assyria, and Armenia. The writing is in all cases both in Chaldæo-Pehlevi and Persian-Pehlevi, of the former of which Sir H. C. Rawlinson copied ten, and of the latter twenty-two portions. In his opinion, the original structure was a fire-temple, on the line of the well-known road from Ctesiphon to the Ecbatana of Atropatene.

The second is the famous bilingual inscription of

Shahpúr at Hajiábád, first noticed and partially copied by Sir Robert K. Porter (vol. i. p. 512). Of this accurate plaister casts were procured nearly forty years ago, by Sir Ephraim Stannus, but till Mr. Thomas took the matter up in 1868, the inscriptions on them had never been sufficiently studied, though printed in more than one work.

If Mr. Thomas be right in the reading he has proposed (and the evidence he has brought forward is to me at least conclusive on this subject), there can be no doubt that in this inscription may be recognized not only the names of our Saviour and of the Jews, but as he justly says "an Eastern paraphrase of portions of our Authorized Version." That the reader may see the translation he has suggested for some portion of this remarkable inscription, I transcribe four lines here, the upper one being that of the Chaldæo-Pehlevi original, the lower that of the Sassanian or Persian. It will be at once seen that they represent the same sense, indeed contain to a great extent the same words:—

Chald. Pehl. "The powerful . . . of the chosen Jews ye (are)."
Sassan. "The supreme Lord of the Jews outside the (ancient) rites he (is)."

Chald. Pehl. "Of a certainty, the Master, the divine Lord," &c.
Sassan. "And, of a certainty, the Master, the divine Lord," &c.

Chald. Pehl. "Created Jews of divine aid, THE Lord, thou."
Sassan. "Lord (Jesus) of divine aid, (the) Lord, he."

Chald. Pehl. "And THE God he (is) great in goodness."
Sassan. "And THE God that (is) God-like, abounding in goodness."

Now we may be quite sure that no one would have

dared to engrave such an inscription on the rock, except by the direct order of Shahpúr himself, and therefore, whether Mr. Thomas' interpretation of it be accepted or not, that it is a promulgation of the religious views of that great monarch. It is quite likely, as suggested by Mr. Thomas, that Shahpúr was much under Western influence after his capture of Valerian, in A.D. 261, at the time, too, when the teaching of Mani, himself a Persian by birth, and originally a Christian presbyter, was making itself felt. We know that Mani after a time had to fly from Persia, and this may not impossibly have been due to the influence he had acquired over the king, which would naturally have aroused the hatred of the fanatical Zoroastrians: moreover, it is certain, that after the decease of Shahpúr, he returned to the Court of his son, Hormazd I., where he was well received and remained for some years.

I here draw to a conclusion such a notice of Ancient Persia as the limit of one small volume has enabled me to bring together; not without the hope, that, though necessarily so brief, the connected story of the three governments who, in succession, ruled over it, may be found interesting and useful.

An Important Historical Series.

EPOCHS OF HISTORY.

EDITED BY

EDWARD E. MORRIS, M.A.,

Each 1 vol. 16mo. with Outline Maps. Price per volume, in cloth, $1.00.

HISTORIES of countries are rapidly becoming so numerous that it is almost impossible for the most industrious student to keep pace with them. Such works are, of course, still less likely to be mastered by those of limited leisure. It is to meet the wants of this very numerous class of readers that the *Epochs of History* has been projected. The series will comprise a number of compact, handsomely printed manuals, prepared by thoroughly competent hands, each volume complete in itself, and sketching succinctly the most important epochs in the world's history, always making the history of a nation subordinate to this more general idea. No attempt will be made to recount all the events of any given period. The aim will be to bring out in the clearest light the salient incidents and features of each epoch. Special attention will be paid to the literature, manners, state of knowledge, and all those characteristics which exhibit the life of a people as well as the policy of their rulers during any period. To make the text more readily intelligible, outline maps will be given with each volume, and where this arrangement is desirable they will be distributed throughout the text so as to be more easy of reference. A series of works based upon this general plan can not fail to be widely useful in popularizing history as science has lately been popularized. Those who have been discouraged from attempting more ambitious works because of their magnitude, will naturally turn to these *Epochs of History* to get a general knowledge of any period; students may use them to great advantage in refreshing their memories and in keeping the true perspective of events, and in schools they will be of immense service as text books,—a point which shall be kept constantly in view in their preparation.

THE FOLLOWING VOLUMES ARE NOW READY:

THE ERA OF THE PROTESTANT REVOLUTION. By F. SEEBOHM, Author of " The Oxford Reformers—Colet, Erasmus, More," with appendix by Prof. GEO. P. FISHER, of Yale College. Author of " HISTORY OF THE REFORMATION."
The CRUSADES. By Rev. G. W. Cox, M.A., Author of the " History of Greece."
The THIRTY YEARS' WAR, 1618—1648. By SAMUEL RAWSON GARDINER.
THE HOUSES OF LANCASTER AND YORK; with the CONQUEST and LOSS of FRANCE. By JAMES GAIRDNER of the Public Record Office. *Now ready.*
THE FRENCH REVOLUTION AND FIRST EMPIRE: an Historical Sketch. By WILLIAM O'CONNOR MORRIS, with an appendix by Hon. ANDREW D. WHITE, President of Cornell University.

☞ *Copies sent post-paid, on receipt of price, by the Publishers.*

ANOTHER GREAT HISTORICAL WORK.

The History of Greece,

By Prof. Dr. ERNST CURTIUS.

Translated by ADOLPHUS WILLIAM WARD, M.A., Fellow of St. Peter's College, Cambridge, Prof. of History in Owen's College, Manchester.

Complete in five vols., crown 8vo, at $2.50 per volume.

PRINTED UPON TINTED PAPER, UNIFORM WITH MOMMSEN'S HISTORY OF ROME, AND THE LIBRARY EDITION OF FROUDE'S HISTORY OF ENGLAND.

Curtius' *History of Greece* is similar in plan and purpose to Mommsen's *History of Rome*, with which it deserves to rank in every respect as one of the great masterpieces of historical literature. Avoiding the minute details which overburden other similar works, it groups together in a very picturesque manner all the important events in the history of this kingdom, which has exercised such a wonderful influence upon the world's civilization. The narrative of Prof. Curtius' work is flowing and animated, and the generalizations, although bold, are philosophical and sound.

CRITICAL NOTICES.

"Professor Curtius' eminent scholarship is a sufficent guarantee for the trustworthiness of his history, while the skill with which he groups his facts, and his effective mode of narrating them, combine to render it no less readable than sound. Professor Curtius everywhere maintains the true dignity and impartiality of history, and it is evident his sympathies are ou the side of justice, humanity, and progress."—*London Athenæum.*

"We can not express our opinion of Dr. Curtius' book better than by saying that it may be fitly ranked with Theodor Mommsen's great work."—*London Spectator.*

"As an introduction to the study of Grecian history, no previous work is comparable to the present for vivacity and picturesque beauty, while in sound learning and accuracy of statement it is not inferior to the elaborate productions which enrich the literature of the age."—*N. Y. Daily Tribune.*

"The History of Greece is treated by Dr. Curtius so broadly and freely in the spirit of the nineteenth century, that it becomes in his hands one of the worthiest and most instructive branches of study for all who desire something more than a knowledge of isolated facts for their education. This translation ought to become a regular part of the accepted course of reading for young men at college, and for all who are in training for the free political life of our country."—*N. Y. Evening Post.*

Sent post-paid, upon receipt of the price, by the Publishers,

SCRIBNER, ARMSTRONG & CO.,
New York.

EDINBURGH REVIEW.—"The **BEST** History of the Roman Republic"
LONDON TIMES.—"BY FAR THE BEST History of the Decline and Fall of the Roman Commonwealth."

THE
History of Rome,

FROM THE EARLIEST TIME TO THE PERIOD OF ITS DECLINE.

By Dr. THEODOR MOMMSEN.

Translated, with the author's sanction and additions, by the Rev. W. P. DICKSON, Regius Professor of Biblical Criticism in the University of Glasgow, late Classical Examiner in the University of St. Andrews. With an Introduction by Dr. LEONHARD SCHMITZ.

REPRINTED FROM THE REVISED LONDON EDITION.

Four Volumes crown 8vo.   **Price per Volume, $2.00.**

Dr. MOMMSEN has long been known and appreciated through his researches into the languages, laws, and institutions of Ancient Rome and Italy, as the most thoroughly versed scholar now living in these departments of historical investigation. To a wonderfully exact and exhaustive knowledge of these subjects, he unites great powers of generalization, a vigorous, spirited, and exceedingly graphic style and keen analytical powers, which give this history a degree of interest and a permanent value possessed by no other record of the decline and fall of the Roman Commonwealth. "Dr. Mommsen's work," as Dr. Schmitz remarks in the introduction, "though the production of a man of most profound and extensive learning and knowledge of the world, is not as much designed for the professional scholar as for intelligent readers of all classes who take an interest in the history of by-gone ages, and are inclined there to seek information that may guide them safely through the perplexing mazes of modern history."

CRITICAL NOTICES.

"A work of the very highest merit; its learning is exact and profound; its narrative full of genius and skill; its descriptions of men are admirably vivid. We wish to place on record our opinion that Dr. Mommsen's is by far the best history of the Decline and Fall of the Roman Commonwealth."—*London Times.*

"Since the days of Niebuhr, no work on Roman History has appeared that combines so much to attract, instruct, and charm the reader. Its style—a rare quality in a German author—is vigorous, spirited, and animated. Professor Mommsen's work can stand a comparison with the noblest productions of modern history."—*Dr. Schmitz.*

Sent post-paid, upon receipt of the price, by the Publishers,

SCRIBNER, ARMSTRONG & CO.,
New York.

EIGHT VOLUMES NOW READY.

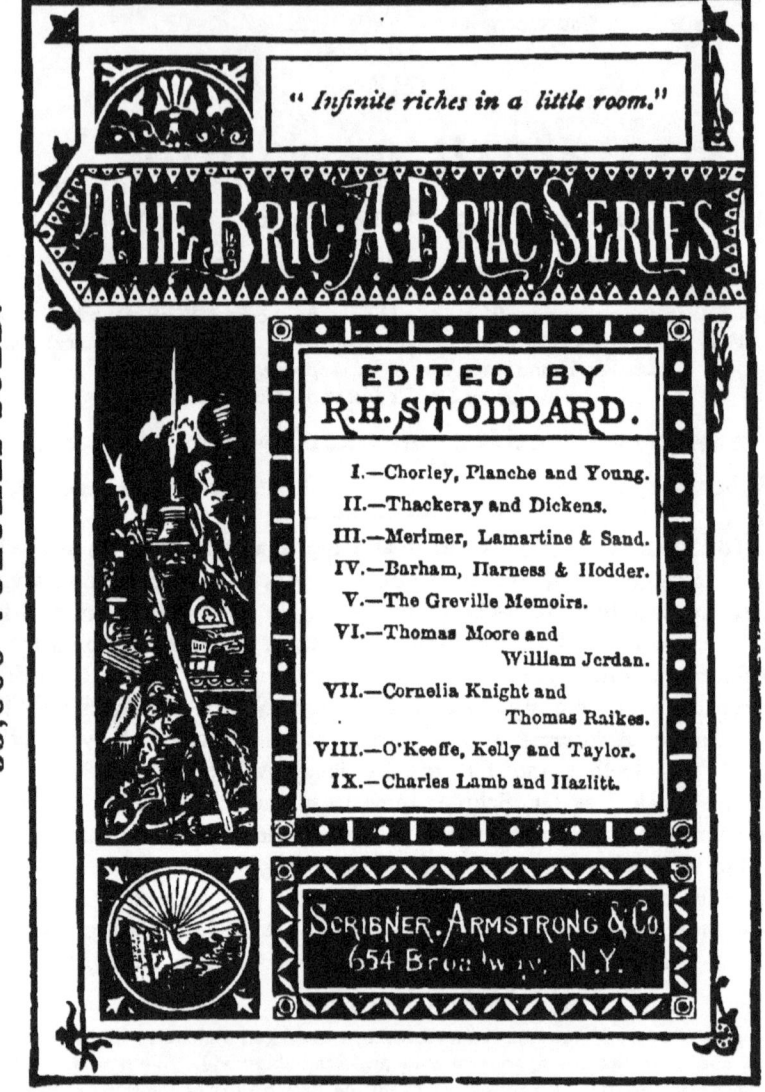

One vol. 12mo, beautifully bound in extra cloth, black and gilt, $1.50.

"No more refreshing volumes could be carried into the country or to the sea-shore, to fill up the niches of time that intervene between the pleasures of the summer holidays."
—*Boston Post.*

"Mr. Stoddard's work appears to be done well nigh perfectly. There is not a dull page in the book."—*N. Y. Evening Post.*

※ SENT POST-PAID, UPON RECEIPT OF PRICE, BY

SCRIBNER, ARMSTRONG & CO., New York.

www.ingramcontent.com/pod-product-compliance
Lightning Source LLC
Chambersburg PA
CBHW020904230426
43666CB00008B/1303